# EMPLOYER HIRING PRACTICES

## Differential Treatment of Hispanic and Anglo Job Seekers

**URBAN INSTITUTE REPORT 90–4**

# Harry Cross, with Genevieve Kenney, Jane Mell, and Wendy Zimmermann

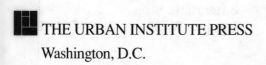

THE URBAN INSTITUTE PRESS

Washington, D.C.

THE URBAN INSTITUTE PRESS
2100 M Street, N.W.
Washington, D.C. 20037

*HD 4903.5 .U58 E47 1990*

*Library of Congress Cataloging in Publication Data*

Employer Hiring Practices: Differential Treatment of Hispanic and Anglo Job Seekers

1. Discrimination in employment--United States.
2. Hispanic American men--Employment--United States.
I. Cross, Harry. II. Series.

HD4903.5.U58E47 ~~1990~~                    90-12115
                                                CIP

(Urban Institute Reports; 90-4  ISSN 0897-7399)

ISBN 0-87766-479-X

Printed in the United States of America.

*Distributed by University Press of America*

| | |
|---|---|
| 4720 Boston Way | 3 Henrietta Street |
| Lanham, MD 20706 | London WC2E 8LU  ENGLAND |

**URBAN INSTITUTE REPORTS** are designed to provide rapid dissemination of research and policy findings. Each report contains timely information and is rigorously reviewed to uphold the highest standards of policy research and analysis.

The Urban Institute is a nonprofit policy research and educational organization established in Washington, D.C., in 1968. Its staff investigates the social and economic problems confronting the nation and government policies and programs designed to alleviate such problems. The Institute disseminates significant findings of its research through the publications program of its Press. The Institute has two goals for work in each of its research areas: to help shape thinking about societal problems and efforts to solve them, and to improve government decisions and performance by providing better information and analytic tools.

Through work that ranges from broad conceptual studies to administrative and technical assistance, Institute researchers contribute to the stock of knowledge available to public officials and private individuals and groups concerned with formulating and implementing more efficient and effective government policy.

Conclusions or opinions expressed in Institute publications are those of the authors and do not necessarily reflect the views of other staff members, officers or trustees of the Institute, advisory groups, or any organizations that provide financial support to the Institute.

# ACKNOWLEDGMENTS

The study on which this report is based was carried out under contract with the General Accounting Office (GAO). The authors would like to thank GAO colleagues Alan Stapleton for his contribution to the research idea and design, and Gail Johnson, Harriet Ganson, and Laurie Ekstrand for their valuable inputs at the pretest and implementation stages of the study. We also appreciate the efforts of Bob Johnson, who was instrumental in conceptualizing and refining our thinking about statistical issues related to hiring audit techniques. We would also like to thank Marc Bendick of Bendick and Egan Economic Consultants for his substantial contribution to the original idea of the research and its design.

We would like to acknowledge the extraordinary performance of the study's testers, who carried out a very complicated research project with great skill and perseverance.

We further appreciate the help and support of our fellow colleagues at The Urban Institute. We especially thank Frank Bean and Michael Fix, who helped originate the idea for this research and contributed to the conceptualization of the research design. Cliff Schrupp, now at the Fair Housing Center of Metropolitan Detroit, furnished the authors with important perspectives on carrying out this type of research, participated enthusiastically in the training, and provided unlimited moral support. Felicity Skidmore and Frank Bean were indispensable critics at the writing stage. Ray Struyk was instrumental in clarifying central theoretical, technical, and organizational issues at key points in the analysis. Edward Bryant provided valuable inputs for the statistical analysis, while Rob Dymowski did a first-rate job of computer programming and analysis.

# CONTENTS

Abstract                                            xi

Preface                                             xiii

Executive Summary                                    1

1   Introduction                                     7

2   Job Vacancy Sampling Program                    11
    Sample Size                                     11
    Types of Jobs                                   12
    The Sampling Frame                              13
    Drawing the Sample                              15

3   Recruitment, Training, and Fieldwork            19
    Recruitment                                     19
    Matching the Testers                            20
    Training                                        21
    Fieldwork                                       24
        Communication                               25
        Technical Procedures                        26

4   Characteristics of Jobs and Employers Audited   29
    Type and Number of Audits                       29
    Types of Ads and Jobs Sampled                   32

| | | |
|---|---|---:|
| | Types of Businesses | 33 |
| | Size of Firms | 36 |
| **5** | **Differences in Treatment** | **39** |
| | Overall Numbers | 40 |
| | Statistical Significance | 46 |
| | Disparate Treatment by Hiring Stage | 50 |
| | Overall Disparate Treatment | 51 |
| | Comparison to Other Studies | 52 |
| | Disparate Treatment by Cities, Occupations, and Businesses | 55 |
| | Qualitative Differences | 57 |
| **6** | **Conclusions** | **61** |
| | Disparate Treatment and Discrimination:  Discussion | 62 |
| | Final Words | 66 |

**Appendices**

| | | |
|---|---|---:|
| **A** | Additional Tables | 69 |
| **B** | Research Design and Tester Training (Table of Contents only) | 91 |

**Bibliography** 93

**Tables**

| | | |
|---|---|---:|
| 4.1 | Types and Number of Audits | 30 |
| 4.2 | Types of Occupations | 34 |
| 4.3 | Types of Businesses | 35 |

4.4   Estimated Size of Company by City          37

5.1   Total Number of Times Testers Reached
        each Stage                                41

5.2   Paired Outcomes by Hiring Stage            45

5.3   Mean Length of Interview by Outcome        59

**Figure**

5.1   Overall Disparate Treatment                53

# ABSTRACT

Discrimination against foreign-looking/sounding citizens in hiring is of particular interest since the 1986 Immigration Reform and Control Act. The broad objective of this study is to ascertain whether foreign-looking/sounding Hispanics are treated differently in the hiring process from those perceived to be U.S. citizens.

In summer 1989, 360 hiring audits on randomly selected employers in Chicago and San Diego were successfully carried out using two-man Hispanic/Anglo teams of young males whose job-related characteristics were carefully matched. The results show that foreign-looking/sounding Hispanics in Chicago and San Diego face considerable barriers compared to their Anglo counterparts in obtaining interviews and offers of employment for low-skilled, entry-level jobs. Specifically,

- Hispanic testers received unfavorable treatment from 3 of every 10 employers;

- Hispanic testers were three times more likely to encounter unfavorable treatment when applying for jobs than similarly qualified Anglos;

- Anglos received 33 percent more interviews than Hispanics;

- Anglos received 52 percent more job offers than Hispanics.

Disparate treatment of Hispanic testers was three times greater than for Anglos. Several caveats that could influence the interpretation of the findings are described. However, it is believed that the methodology employed in the study may yield a lower bound estimate of the amount of disparate treatment. In sum, the study documents sizeable disparity in the treatment of Hispanic and Anglo testers in Chicago and San Diego. The authors believe that a significant portion of this disparate treatment is the result of discrimination.

This study was designed and implemented in collaboration with the General Government Division of the General
Accounting Office (GAO). The hiring audit is one of
several methods used by the GAO to respond to its
congressional mandate to investigate the discrimination
effects of the Employer Sanctions Provision of the 1986
Immigration Reform and Control Act (IRCA). It is the
only one in the series of GAO studies of IRCA-related
discrimination not carried out directly by GAO, and it
differs from the other studies in that it uses direct rather
than indirect observation to measure employer hiring
behavior. The findings of this hiring audit will be
incorporated into the last of three reports on IRCA-related
discrimination that the GAO is required to submit to
Congress.

The Urban Institute in collaboration with GAO staff
developed and tested the hiring audit methodology,
implemented it in two cities in summer 1989, and analyzed
the results. The GAO funded preparation of the final
research design, fieldwork, and data analysis. The Urban
Institute provided support for the initial research design
and experts to participate as needed in the study activities.

The research carried out for this study pertained to
several questions regarding disparate treatment in hiring
and IRCA-related hiring procedures. This particular

report focuses on the issues of whether or not there are differences in how far Hispanic job applicants go in the hiring process compared to those perceived to be U.S. citizens. The findings of this study, taken alone, are not a measure of hiring discrimination resulting from IRCA employer sanctions. The relationship of these findings to IRCA employer sanctions has been analyzed by the GAO in its third report to Congress (1990) in tandem with the GAO's other studies.

This study makes frequent reference to a supporting document, Appendix B, which includes technical memos, forms used for data collection, and the training manual. Appendix B contains twelve sections, referred to as B-1 through B-12. This appendix appears in the full study, which in the form it was submitted to the GAO, is available through The Urban Institute's Publications Office under the title "Differential Treatment Between Hispanic and Anglo Job Seekers: A Study of Hiring Practices in Two Cities," Cross et al., November 1989.

Discrimination against foreign-looking/ sounding citizens in hiring is of particular interest since the 1986 Immigration Reform and Control Act (IRCA), which forbids discrimination against authorized workers on the basis of citizenship or national origin. Although studies have been conducted on disparate treatment in the housing market for blacks and whites and for Hispanics and Anglos, little comparable work has been done on disparate treatment in hiring of Hispanics and Anglos. This hiring audit study is the first of its kind in the United States. The broad objective of the study is to ascertain whether foreign-looking/sounding Hispanics and those perceived to be U.S. citizens (Anglos) are treated differently in the hiring process when both groups have similar qualifications. The study helps answer the following specific research questions:

1. Are there differences in how far foreign-looking/ sounding Hispanic job applicants go in the hiring process as compared to those perceived to be U.S. citizens?

2. Are there differences in the numbers of job applications, interviews, and offers obtained by

foreign-looking/sounding Hispanic applicants as compared to those appearing to be citizens?

To answer these questions, in summer 1989 a hiring audit was conducted on randomly selected employers in two cities--Chicago and San Diego. Trained, male college students in their early twenties served as matched Hispanic and Anglo testers who were similarly qualified in key job-related characteristics. Considerable time was spent on tester training, and controls were introduced for the quantity and quality of educational background, work experience, age, citizenship (all were U.S. citizens), physical condition, availability, fluency in English, dress, height, weight, salary desired, demeanor, etc. A total of 360 audits were carried out successfully by eight two-man Hispanic/Anglo teams.

The study chose to sample low-skilled, entry-level jobs where the bulk of young Hispanic adults begin their working careers. These include jobs in hotel, restaurant and other services, retail sales, office work, management (mainly trainee positions), technical areas, and general labor, including manufacturing. Since disparate treatment of Hispanics at the entry level can compound the adverse effect on upward mobility, identifying and eliminating entry-level barriers facing Hispanic job seekers could pro-vide the greatest leverage in improving their employment opportunities. Newspaper help-wanted ads offered the most promise for a sound sampling methodology for reasons that are elaborated. However, using newspaper ads for the sample frame may provide a lower bound estimate of disparate treatment because employers who advertise in newspapers tend to discriminate less than those who hire through personal contact and direct application.

The results show that foreign-looking/sounding Hispanics in San Diego and Chicago face considerable barriers compared to their Anglo counterparts in obtaining interviews and offers of employment for low-skilled, entry-level jobs. Specifically,

- Hispanic testers received unfavorable treatment from 3 of every 10 employers;

- Hispanic testers were three times more likely to encounter unfavorable treatment when applying for jobs than similarly qualified Anglos;

- Anglos received 33 percent more interviews than Hispanics; and

- Anglos received 52 percent more job offers than Hispanics.

The study found dramatic differences in the employment outcomes of matched Hispanic/Anglo pairs. Hispanic testers received unfavorable treatment in 31 percent of the audits, while the Anglo testers received unfavorable treatment in only 11 percent of the audits. Thus, disparate treatment for Hispanic testers was three times greater than for Anglos. Several caveats should be noted when interpreting these findings. First, other characteristics relevant to employer decisions, if correlated with the testers' ethnicity, could bias the finding on disparate treatment related to ethnicity. However, given the controls for educational background, work experience, age, and so on, it is difficult to imagine that these types of factors could lead to the large amounts of disparate treatment found in this study.

Second, these audits covered only a subset of jobs and employers in two cities and were carried out only by young male testers. The amount of disparate treatment found may not be representative of that found in other cities or for Hispanics who are older, female, have heavier accents, or are less ethnic-appearing. Depending on the group used as testers, levels of disparate treatment could be lower or higher. However, the two cities selected for the audit have a measure of regional representativeness.

Third, the types of jobs sampled underrepresent the technical and manufacturing occupations, since about three-quarters of the jobs sampled were in sales and services. However, the majority of these jobs are among the fastest growing or will provide the largest number of new jobs in the 1990s. Therefore, though the jobs audited constitute only a subset in two cities, they nevertheless represent a large portion of the job market facing young Hispanics between now and the year 2000.

Fourth, disparate treatment can result from systematic behavior, such as discrimination, or from random events such as an employer's bad mood. It is possible that disparate treatment is entirely related to systematic behavior, random events, or a combination of both. The method used for this study subtracts unfavorable treatment of Anglos from unfavorable treatment of Hispanics to arrive at "net disparate treatment." The assumption underlying this method is that random events are cancelled out by the subtraction and that the residual accounts for systematic behavior only. This approach assumes that random unfavorable treatment is symmetrical for Anglo and Hispanic outcomes. Some researchers believe that this approach results in a lower estimate of the amount of disparate treatment accounted for by systematic behavior, but the reverse is also possible.

These caveats do not change the fact that about one-third of the time, similarly qualified Hispanic job seekers in this study were treated less favorably than young Anglo job seekers. In sum, the study documents sizeable disparities in the treatment of Hispanic and Anglo testers in Chicago and San Diego. The authors believe that a significant portion of this disparate treatment is the result of discrimination.

# Chapter One

# INTRODUCTION

Studies have documented that Hispanic men have higher unemployment rates and lower wage levels compared to their Anglo counterparts (Cain 1986; Reimers 1985; Defreitas 1985). These differences have persisted over time and their cumulative effect may have resulted in worsening economic conditions for Hispanics over the last 10 years. Bureau of the Census data suggest that the number of Hispanics living in poverty continues to increase, and reached 27 percent in 1988, compared to a national average of 13 percent (Broder, 1989).

It is not clear what role labor force discrimination plays in explaining the unemployment levels and lower earnings among Hispanics. Researchers have tried to assess the extent of discrimination through quantitative, multivariate analyses of unemployment and wages. These studies attempt to control for a host of personal characteristics that are potentially related to productivity, such as education, age, and language ability. Researchers then assess what proportion of the wage or employment gap can be attributable to differences between Hispanics and Anglos in these personal characteristics. They have found, for example, that the significantly lower educational attainment of Hispanics relative to Anglos explains a large portion of the differential. The portion that is not explained by differences in relevant personal characteristics, or the residual, is then attributed to labor force discrimination or to differences in unmeasured characteristics. Using this method, Defreitas (1985) found that together, discrimination and unmeasured characteristics could account for roughly one-third of the higher unemployment rates observed among Hispanic men.

This Urban Institute study is the first hiring audit study in the United States. It was conducted to investigate the possible discrimination effects of the employer sanctions provision of the 1986 Immigration Reform and Control Act (IRCA). This provision requires employers to comply with the law by having employees fill out a work eligibility form and by examining employees' documents. Hispanics were chosen for the audit because both Congress and minority interest groups felt this segment of the population was at the greatest risk of discrimination as a result of IRCA.

The study breaks new ground by using for the first time an audit approach for employment. This technique has been used successfully in housing discrimination audits, which were first conducted in the late 1970s (Wienk et al. 1979; Hakken 1979). When applied to employment, the methodology involves direct observation of disparate treatment by employers in the hiring process. The audit approach offers a particularly powerful method of analysis because it permits control over employer and job seeker characteristics, diminishing the possibility that unmeasured characteristics explain any differences that emerge.

Specifically, this hiring audit compares the treatment of "U.S.-looking" citizens (i.e., Anglos with no foreign accents) with that of "foreign-looking/sounding" citizens (i.e., Hispanics fluent in English with accents) under partially controlled conditions. It compares the job market outcomes of 360 hiring audits on randomly selected employers in Chicago and San Diego. The audits were conducted through eight two-man Hispanic/Anglo teams whose job-related characteristics were carefully matched.

The success of this hiring audit study has several important policy implications. First, the methodology used for this audit might be adopted as a tool for monitoring or possibly enforcing equal employment laws for any minority group. Second, if replicated in other sites and for other Hispanic sub-groups, the methodology can tell us the extent to which the study's findings can be generalized. Third, the findings indicate that Hispanics may indeed be facing discrimination in the labor market, which may call for policy and programmatic responses beyond those now in existence.

# Chapter Two

# JOB VACANCY SAMPLING PLAN

Sampling required decisions on three major components:
1) sample size; 2) types of jobs, and therefore employers,
to be sampled; and 3) the sampling frame from which the
jobs and employers were to be selected.

## *SAMPLE SIZE*

The sample size decision was constrained by the absence of
prior experience in hiring audits (making cost estimates
difficult), a fixed and limited budget, lack of knowledge
about the extent of disparate treatment of Hispanic job
applicants, and the consensus of the advisory group that
the study include hiring audits in two distinct geographic
regions.

Our best estimates, confirmed in the pretest, indicated
that the budget could accommodate a maximum sample
size of 400 audits. Allowing for tester dropouts and
nonresponse from the audits, we calculated that the study
could deliver 300-350 valid audits in a period of five to six
weeks using eight pairs of testers working full time. The
number of testers was limited to four pairs in each city to
permit efficient use of financial and supervisory personnel,

in-depth individual training and practice before the audit began, an opportunity for closely matching the pairs, and adequate control by the site managers over the quality and scheduling of work. The use of full-time testers yielded a group of experienced testers after the first week of the study. A larger number of testers working part time would have reduced the effectiveness of both training and matching, and would have increased the time needed for them to become experienced.

Before undertaking the hiring audit, we analyzed the level of statistical precision that could be expected for estimates from a cluster sample of 300 to 400 audits. Our analysis relied on variance estimates associated with the normal test of paired differences. The cluster nature of the sample arose because each of the eight matched pairs was to carry out multiple audits. We determined that a net difference in treatment of 15 percent or more could be detected--at a significance level of 5 percent and a power level of 95 percent--for moderate values of the intra-cluster correlation coefficient when favorable treatment for Anglos and Hispanics combined is 40 percent or less (see Cross 1989, and Appendix B-3 for fuller discussion).

## *TYPES OF JOBS*

The study chose to sample low-skilled, entry-level jobs requiring limited experience because these jobs are typically filled by high school graduates in the 20-24 age range. They have been called generic entry-level jobs (Bendick 1988), and include occupations in hotel, restaurant and other services, retail sales, office work, management (mainly trainee positions), technical areas, and general labor, including manufacturing. (A list of the types of occupations eligible for sampling in this study is found in Appendix B-8.) *These occupations represent precisely the types of jobs where the bulk of Hispanic young adults begin their working careers.* Since disparate treatment toward Hispanics *at the entry level* can compound the adverse effect on upward mobility, identifying and eliminating entry-level barriers facing Hispanic job seekers could provide leverage in improving their employment opportunities.

Not all low-skilled, entry-level jobs were appropriate for this study. Numerous jobs were judged to be ineligible for sampling because they required such credentials as special driver's licenses or equipment such as a tool chest. Other jobs ineligible for this study include part-time, temporary, commission-only sales jobs, or government positions. Similarly excluded are jobs filled through intermediaries such as employment services, and jobs for which a foreign language is a bona fide occupational qualification. These and a number of other exclusions are listed in Appendix B-9. One of the more important practical exclusions eliminated jobs located more than 15 miles from the project office in each city.

## THE SAMPLING FRAME

The principal requirement for drawing a random sample is that the universe be defined so that each of the job vacancies in the selected occupations has an equal chance of being drawn. This proved to be a major constraint for the study (see Appendix B-2, Cross/Stapleton Memo, 4/21/89).

The literature and statistics on job search methods in the United States suggest that most jobs are obtained through 1) personal contacts (friends, relatives), 2) direct application, and 3) intermediaries such as newspaper ads and employment services (Holzer 1987). We assessed the possibilities of sampling all these main methods.

Sampling through personal contacts proved impossible because the informality precludes the possibility of defining a universe of job openings. Sampling direct application also proved to be impossible. Direct application can be divided into the "plant gate" approach in which job seekers make unsolicited applications to employers, and the "help wanted" approach in which applicants respond to signs and notices in employers' windows. No one as yet has been able to define the universe of direct application job vacancies, so we were precluded from drawing a random sample of this method. (See Appendix B-2, Cross/Stapleton Memo, 4/21/89, for fuller discussion of direct application sampling possibilities.)

Elimination of personal contact and direct application methods left intermediary channels as the only source for a random sampling frame. Of all the sources in this category, newspaper help-wanted ads offered the most promise for a sound sampling methodology. The following are the principal advantages of using newspapers in a short-term hiring audit:

- Newspaper ads are one of the main sources of employment information used by young adults. Surveys show that 30 percent to 60 percent of young adults use newspaper help-wanted ads as a job search method (Bureau of Labor Statistics 1989; Holzer 1988).

- Newspaper ads, particularly for sales, services, clerical and blue collar jobs, are roughly representative of the distribution of all job vacancies in broad occupational categories (Abraham 1987).

- For a single source, newspaper help-wanted ads provide centralized access to a large number of jobs. In large city newspapers, thousands of ads appear every weekend. These ads are relatively simple to sample.

- Newspaper ads serve as a productive, low-cost approach for a hiring audit because each ad represents an employer who is presumably ready to make a job hiring decision, in contrast to direct application where employers often let applications languish without any progress or resolution.

- It is known how job seekers and employers use newspaper ads.

- Employers who advertise in the newspaper tend to discriminate less than those who hire through personal contact and direct application. Thus, a newspaper help-wanted ad sampling frame is likely to provide lower bound estimates of any disparate treatment (see Appendix B-2, U.I. Team/Stapleton Memo, 9/28/89).

---

## DRAWING THE SAMPLE

Random samples of job vacancies were drawn from the Sunday help-wanted sections of the *Chicago Tribune* (Sunday circulation: 1,138,731) and the *San Diego Union* (Sunday circulation: 342,000). Each Sunday during the fieldwork period the site managers drew the sample for the following week. First they assigned a sequential number to each qualifying ad. Then, using random numbers tables, they selected the ads (and the employers they represented) for auditing by the tester pairs. About two-thirds of all ads contained announcements for more than one job vacancy. When this occurred, the site manager assigned the ad two numbers. This procedure effectively doubled the probability that a two-job ad would be selected, thus maintaining the equal selection probabilities. Site managers were able to initiate audits on 40 to 50 viable ads per week.

During the audit it was discovered that roughly one-third of the ads did not lead to audits. This "nonresponse" rate was principally due to three factors: jobs had already been taken, testers could not make contact with the employers, or both testers were screened out on the phone. (For fuller discussion of employer nonresponse, see Appendix B-3, Zimmermann/Cross Memo, 10/10/89.)

The nonresponse rate for this study has important implications for future work in hiring audits that use newspaper help-wanted ads. Expanding the scope of the study beyond 40-50 audits per week would require either 1) an additional source of ads (i.e., another newspaper), or 2) tester pairs with higher qualifications that would reduce exclusions and increase the size of the sample frame.

Some qualifications about generalizing from the results of this sampling approach are worth discussing. The first is that our sample provides information on disparate treatment for just two cities. Hiring audits in two cities are not sufficient to justify broad generalized statements about disparate treatment in the U.S. However, the two cities are located in different regions of the U.S., and thus have, by definition, some measure of regional representativeness. San Diego, for example, is similar in ethnic make-up, economy, physical configuration, and proximity to Mexico, to many other areas of the Southwest (e.g., Phoenix, Arizona; San Bernardino, California; Orange County, California; Long Beach, California, etc.). Chicago is the "capital" of the midwest, and has economic similarities to urban areas such as St. Louis, Missouri, Gary, Indiana, and Milwaukee, Wisconsin, which are far from the Mexican border.

The second qualification is that the sample drawn is only a subset of jobs and employers in each city. But there are some characteristics of jobs that suggest the results could have applicability beyond the subset of jobs sampled. Later, we shall see that the sub-set of jobs sampled in this study are where many of today's employment opportunities are for young adult job seekers.

The third qualification is that because the study uses newspaper ads for the sample frame, we believe it may provide a lower bound estimate of disparate treatment for these two cities because advertisers in the newspaper media tend to discriminate less.

# Chapter Three

## RECRUITMENT, TRAINING, AND FIELDWORK

College students were chosen as the tester group because of the belief that they could readily grasp the hiring audit methodology and could be trained effectively in a short period of time. The Chicago pretest confirmed both beliefs. Furthermore, college students could be rapidly recruited in just a few locations, and were available for a six-week summer job. Finally, college students are in the right age cohort (20-24), and most of them have had some work experience in the kinds of jobs to be audited in the study.

### *RECRUITMENT*

Recruitment took place on the campuses of major colleges and universities in the San Diego and Chicago areas. Project team members consulted with placement offices, faculty, and other researchers to identify applicants. Approximately 40 applicants were either screened by phone or interviewed in each location. The site managers and project director made the selection. Principal selection criteria included applicants' research orientation, acting ability, credibility as average job seekers, personal documentation, obvious national origin appearance and speech, and potential to be matched to another tester (see Appendix B-6, Zimmermann/Cross Memo, 6/29/89, for further information on tester selection). Testers of exceptional qualifications or enthusiasm, and their opposites, were excluded during the selection process to reduce the impact of tester characteristics on the outcome.

The 16 testers ultimately selected were for the most part social science students from the following colleges: University of Chicago, University of Illinois at Chicago, Northeastern University, DePaul University, Northwestern University, The University of California at San Diego, San Diego State University, Southwestern Community College, and The University of California at Berkeley.

---

## MATCHING THE TESTERS

The matching of young job seekers to form two-person Hispanic/Anglo teams involved objective and subjective evaluation. The objective criteria were relatively simple and included age, weight, height, ethnicity, possession of driver's licences, and work history. Subjective criteria included creativity, communication ability, grasp of the methodology, ability to carry out objective research, accent, overall demeanor, and appearance.

The matching of the pairs occurred in several phases and involved a number of persons. The first assessment for matching took place during the interview phase, when site managers, local consultants and advisors made initial judgments about the characteristics of applicants.

The second phase of matching occurred during the first day of tester training, after testers had been observed closely by the project director, the site managers, GAO personnel, and an outside housing audit expert. Each observer made an independent match of the pairs during this first day. The group then discussed their suggested matchings and reached consensus on the best paired testers. Tester comparability was a key criterion in matching decisions. Because of the careful culling of applicants at the first stage, the observers were close to identical in their selection of pairs.

The final matching phase occurred at the end of the three-day training period. The observation groups again discussed the matching to determine whether the initial matchings were still valid after two more days of training, role playing, and actual experience, which was incorporated into the training process. No switching of pairs was found necessary at this stage.

---

## TRAINING

Tester training had to accomplish two key objectives: 1) assure that all controllable tester variables were held constant; and 2) assure that testers learned to follow all scheduling and data collection procedures. Controlling tester variables focused on two aspects of our surrogate job applicants. The first involved the testers' tangible characteristics such as clothing, age, education, and work history. The second involved nontangible characteristics such as level of enthusiasm and spontaneous responses to questions.

A four-person team trained the eight testers in each city. Team members included the project director, the site manager, a senior technical professional from the GAO in Washington, D.C., and the director of field operations of the largest housing audit ever undertaken in the United States. (The results of this joint study, funded by HUD and conducted by The Urban Institute and Syracuse University, will be available in late 1990.) Because of the high ratio of trainers to testers, each tester received considerable individual attention during training.

Tester training occupied two-and-a-half days in each city. Prior to training, testers read portions of the research design and studied the training manual composed for the study (see Appendix B-12). After the testers gained a thorough understanding of the project's objectives, implementation, and data collection activities, each tester worked with the project team to modify his personal history to fit the profile of the average young adult job seeker. The generic profile of this study's typical job applicant can be found in the research design (Cross 1989). The objective in modifying biographies was to make the testers as comparable as possible to their partners. Testers generally kept their own birthdates, home addresses, social security numbers, driver's licenses, and other basic information. Modifications were made for educational attainment levels, citizenship and birthplace in certain cases, hobbies, and work experience. Personal and past job references were simulated.

In modifying biographies, the project team attempted to retain as much of the real experience of the testers as possible. This approach made it easier for testers to remember their biographies and to answer questions during interviews. However, for some testers it was necessary to alter some of their key biographical information. When the modifications were complete, the project had 16 testers with equivalent personal information, work and educational histories, and references.

The average tester had the following tangible characteristics: male, 22 years old, U.S. citizen, high school graduate, neatly dressed, no criminal record, one or two semesters of course credit at a community college, and work experience for a year or two each as a stockperson and a waiter. The only difference in the absolute characteristics among our testers were national origin and accent. All Hispanics had slight Spanish accents, dark hair, and light brown skin. None of the Anglos had accents and all had brown, blonde, or red hair, and white skin. Testers in both groups were well-spoken and intelligent. (For a complete simulated biography of each of the 16 testers in this hiring audit, see Appendix B-10.)

All project testers were trained to seek the highest advancement potential and the highest pay. Project team members also trained the testers in nontangible aspects of the hiring process. These included demeanor, courtesy, and responses to employer questions. In intensive working sessions, testers practiced answering questions new backgrounds, career goals, reasons for wanting to change jobs, work experience, where they lived, references, and so on. They participated in role playing and simulated interviews, and practiced filling out applications. Testers worked closely with their matched partners throughout the training, observing one another answering a variety of interview and phone questions. Testers also received continuous feedback from the trainers and fellow testers on their performances. By the end of training, the two members of the matched tester teams were adept at answering typical interview questions with similar levels of enthusiasm, length of response, and demeanor. Training ended with a series of actual phone calls and direct application visits to employers to complete applications, seek interviews, and interact with potential employers. Through this exercise, pairs had further opportunities to learn similar behaviors.

---

## FIELDWORK

Fieldwork in the two cities was undertaken concurrently over a period of five consecutive weeks during July and August 1989. Because many of the job applications required two weeks to obtain valid outcomes, about 90 percent of the audits were initiated on the Mondays and Tuesdays of the first four weeks. The tester pairs needed to complete an average of 10 audits per week to reach the desired target for each city sample size.

Valid audits were defined in the research design as any in which the employer had the opportunity to make a choice to give an interview or a job offer to either or both of the testers. Stated in another way, an audit was judged valid if one or both of the testers filled out an application and had subsequent contact with the employer. This definition of valid audit assured that all audits used in the study provided employers the chance to make a job-relevant decision about the tester pair. (Information on help-wanted ads that were selected for inclusion in the study but did not result in valid audits is given in Appendix B-3.)

In carrying out the fieldwork, the project team discovered that 10 to 12 hiring audits per pair per week was about the maximum that could be undertaken. Several factors limit the "audit productivity" of tester pairs. First, not all audits initiated result in valid audits. Testers may spend some time seeking to meet with employers without success, and are not always able to have contact with employers after the application has been filled out. Second, audits necessarily overlap from one week to the next. After the first week, testers are initiating new job applications while still scheduling interviews and calls from the prior week's audits. Testers' time schedules, therefore, cannot accommodate more than about 10 audits a week without encountering the risk of being unresponsive to employer requests for interviews and meetings.

From the implementation standpoint, the scheduling and tracking of tester activities are the most critical features of hiring audit fieldwork. Proper timing and careful follow-up are essential. Site managers accomplished timely scheduling and tracking by using a series of pretested forms. These forms included a master schedule to track the separate stages of each audit, tester assignment forms, phone logs to record messages from employers, and survey instruments with a cover sheet to facilitate audit scheduling and tracking by individual testers (see Appendix B-11 for examples of these forms). Testers also carried their own individual appointment books for scheduling activities. Using these forms and tracking systems was key to the success of the hiring audit.

## Communication

Project team members placed a high value on continuous communication during implementation of the audit. Testers made an average of three phone calls a day to the site manager and visited the project office an average of once a day. Site managers maintained daily communication with the project director. The project director visited each city three times during the audit, and GAO personnel visited each site twice for monitoring purposes. Emphasis on communication meant that sample selection, tester activities, and data collection were closely managed and tracked. Site managers were personally able to review each tester's survey instruments daily, record individual tester progress, confirm that appointments and phone calls had been made, and provide round-the-clock guidance to testers. The project director and GAO personnel, in turn, provided direct feedback for problems requiring immediate attention, and worked closely with site managers and testers on refining technical procedures.

## Technical Procedures

Besides close communication, several other principles guided implementation of the fieldwork.

First, in order to provide each tester in a pair with an equal opportunity to receive an interview or job offer, any tester with a job offer immediately turned it down. Trainers provided guidance and practice to testers during role-playing sessions so that turning down offers was carried out easily and without stress. In the majority of cases, testers turned down job offers on the spot, either on the telephone (responding to employers' telephone offers) or at the end of the interview. Occasionally testers could not refuse the offer immediately. They would say they had to "think it over" or "check on another possibility." Several hours later they would call back to turn down the job, thus keeping open the opportunity for their partners to receive a job offer.

Second, testers initiated their audits within specified time frames. For help-wanted ads requesting an initial phone call, matched testers made their calls within 30 minutes of each other. More common was for pair members to make calls within 10 minutes of each other.

For help-wanted ads requesting a personal visit by the applicant, matched testers scheduled their arrivals within 15 to 60 minutes of each other. This close timing is critical to the hiring audit, because it is the only way to ensure that the employer begins his/her consideration of the testers at about the same time, thus minimizing the danger that intervening events would distort the employer's consideration of the audit's two applicants. Of course, it is not possible to control for the number and characteristics of other "real" job seekers whose job applications may affect employers' decisions regarding the tester applicants.

Third, site managers assigned testers to be either the "initial" applicant or the "comparison" applicant, and the two members of each tester pair alternated in making the first call or visit to the employer. Alternating in this manner ensured that random events would not cause either the Anglos or the Hispanics to be disproportionately first or second to apply and thus possibly influence the outcomes.

Finally, to ensure consistent data collection testers were required to fill out their survey instruments immediately after each stage in the hiring process. Testers filled out the survey pertaining to the initial phone call immediately after hanging up the phone, and filled out the sections on interviews in their cars or on the bus immediately after the interview. Site managers reviewed tester surveys on a daily basis to ensure completeness and to deal with any ambiguities in tester observations (e.g., interpretations of questions on applications regarding documents or eligibility to work).

Once a tester pair completed an audit, the site manager reviewed the two audits for completeness and inconsistencies. Inconsistencies were resolved in weekly meetings with the audit pairs. The site manager then filled out a "valid audit checklist" and a "valid audit comparison" form to certify that the survey had been completed satisfactorily and that all procedures had been followed.  At this stage, valid audits were also categorized as complete, terminated, or truncated (see below).  Finally, during site visits the project director reviewed all tracking forms and completed audits, and was onsite for the last week of each city audit to conduct the final reviews with the site managers.

# Chapter Four

# CHARACTERISTICS OF JOBS AND EMPLOYERS AUDITED

## *TYPES AND NUMBER OF AUDITS*

Five weeks of fieldwork in Chicago and San Diego resulted in a total of 360 valid audits. Valid audits take three forms in this study: completed, terminated, and truncated. The distinctions among them are important for interpreting the findings. The three types of valid audits by city are found in table 4.1 below.

The majority of valid audits (84 percent) were seen through to their logical conclusion and are called "completed valid audits." That is, the employer was able to give the testers full consideration after one or both of them filled out an application. A key determinant of a complete audit was the amount of time that had passed since the initial contact with the employer. The study found that 95 percent of all employers made interview or job offer decisions within a three-week period. In 302 of our audits, the employers had sufficient time to make decisions regarding our testers. In these 302 cases, therefore, project testers had a full opportunity to be hired.

Another 5 percent of the valid audits had to be terminated before one or both testers had the opportunity to receive a job offer. Terminated audits occurred when

Table 4.1  TYPES AND NUMBER OF AUDITS

|  | Chicago | San Diego | Total | (%) |
|---|---|---|---|---|
| Completed | 142 | 160 | 302 | (84) |
| Valid audits; neither terminated nor truncated | | | | |
| Terminated | 9 | 10 | 19 | (5) |
| Valid audits terminated because of unexpected events | | | | |
| Truncated | 18 | 21 | 39 | (11) |
| Valid audits started in last two weeks of study where an employer did not make a job offer decision for at least one tester | | | | |
| TOTALS | 169 | 191 | 360 | (100) |

testers were forced to withdraw their applications because an unexpected event intervened in the hiring process. An example of a terminated audit is when a tester met a neighbor at the employer's office, or the tester was asked to take a personality test after an interview. The audit was only counted as a valid terminated audit if these unexpected events did not occur until after the employer had the opportunity to make an interview decision for *both* testers. If unexpected events occurred *before* this point, the audits were considered invalid.

The remaining 11 percent of the valid audits were truncated by the end of the fieldwork period, but had progressed far enough so that the employers had at least the opportunity to make a decision about interviewing both testers. These audits--all begun in the last two weeks of the project--would have been complete audits had there been enough time for the employer to make final job decisions. Because the employer did at least have the opportunity to offer interviews to the testers, they are counted as valid audits.

All 360 valid audits are included in the analysis of treatment at the *application* and *interview* stages, since employers had an opportunity to make these decisions in all cases. Only 302 audits are included in the analysis of treatment at the *job offer* stage because the other 58 audits were terminated or truncated before the employers had the chance to make a hiring decision about both testers. Thus the sample size (n) for applications and interviews is 360, and the sample size for job offers is 302. The sample size for overall analysis of the three hiring stages together is 360.

Although the proportions of completed, terminated, and truncated audits are similar in both cities (see table 4.1), the total number of audits by city differ by 22 even though an identical effort was expended in each location. The reason for the difference in numbers of valid audits obtained for each city can be attributed to the difference in the number of ads for entry-level, low-skilled labor in each city's major newspaper. This probably reflects differences underlying the availability of those types of jobs in each site. The *San Diego Union*, serving a metropolitan area of slightly less than 2 million people, contained more help-wanted ads for low-skilled jobs than the *Chicago Tribune*, which serves a metropolitan area of more than 7 million people. Furthermore, the "nonresponse" rate of ads in

Chicago was much higher than in San Diego, possibly due to differences in labor availability (see Appendix B-3, Zimmermann/Mell/Cross Memo, 10/16/89). At the time of the fieldwork, there was a considerable difference in overall city unemployment rates between San Diego and Chicago--4.8 percent and 6.5 percent, respectively, in July 1989 (U.S. Department of Labor 1989).

The availability of viable help-wanted ads is critical to a hiring audit that uses newspaper ads as its sample frame. Designers of future hiring audits will want to make sure that the cities selected have sufficient demand for low-skilled labor, that the time frame for the study is comparable with the number of viable help-wanted ads, and that the sample frame can be expanded if necessary.

---

## TYPES OF ADS AND JOBS SAMPLED

In the sampling discussion, we noted that numerous ads announced more than one job, and that these ads were oversampled. In fact, the large majority of ads used in the study (66 percent) advertised the availability of two or more jobs eligible for the sample. This fact is important because it reduces the potential dependent outcome effects of two testers competing directly for the same position. This is discussed in the beginning of chapter 5.

The weekly sampling included a variety of occupations. They ranged from ordinary service jobs, such as waiter or busboy, to somewhat less ordinary jobs, such as ticket seller in a circus. Although 86 percent of the jobs offered wages between $3.75 to $7.50 per hour, most offered the job seeker an opportunity to start a career and move up in the company, or to increase his wages in a short period of time. About 1 in 20 of the jobs were entry-level management positions with clear opportunities for advancement in the company. For example, in various of the retail jobs, employers would mention the possibility of becoming a shift manager, assistant manager, or even store manager.

The types of occupations included in the sample have been divided into eight categories as depicted in table 4.2. The largest category of occupations sampled in the study is service jobs. This is not surprising since among all U.S. sectors, the service sector has been growing the fastest in the past 15 years and has displayed the greatest demand in urban areas. In our sample, service jobs accounted for 56 percent of the occupations--57 percent in Chicago and 53 percent in San Diego. Retail sales occupations constituted the next largest category in the sample, accounting for 16 percent of the total number of jobs. Together, service and sales jobs accounted for almost three-quarters of the total number of occupations.

Office, general labor, technical and management occupations make up the remainder of the sample. The only noteworthy difference between the two cities is in the general labor category, which was 13 percent in San Diego and only 5 percent in Chicago. These occupations fell mainly in construction and heavy labor businesses such as landscaping. It is possible that this difference can be attributed to California's real estate and building boom of the late 1980s (Rudnitsky 1989).

---

## TYPES OF BUSINESSES

The audit covered a wide range of businesses, which are categorized by the definitions used by the Census Bureau

Table 4.2  TYPES OF OCCUPATIONS (percentage of audits)

| | Chicago | San Diego | Total |
|---|---|---|---|
| **Services** | | | |
| Hotel | 10 | 10 | 10 |
| Other | 20 | 25 | 23 |
| Restaurant | 27 | 18 | 23 |
| Total | 57 | 53 | 56 |
| Sales | 19 | 14 | 16 |
| Office | 11 | 9 | 10 |
| General labor | 5 | 13 | 9 |
| Technical | 2 | 8 | 5 |
| Management | 6 | 3 | 4 |

Note: Based on N=360. Categories were derived from job titles listed in ads sampled.

in its Economic Censuses.  Table 4.3 shows the hiring audit figures by types of businesses.

To simplify the categories for this study, the Census Bureau's divisions were condensed into retail trade, service, wholesale trade, manufacturers, and construction. The hiring audit sample was dominated by retail trade and service businesses.  Retail businesses constituted the largest group of audited employers, nearly half (46 percent) of the total.  Within this group, "eating and drinking places" made up nearly half of the retail subtotal and 21 percent of the total sample of businesses.  The second largest category, "services," consisted mainly of hotels, business services firms, and "other" (warehouses, electronics, communications, etc.).  These made up 41 percent of the sample of employers.  The remaining 13 percent were in wholesale trade and manufacturing.

Table 4.3    TYPES OF BUSINESS
(percentage of audits)

|  | Chicago | San Diego | Total |
|---|---|---|---|
| Retail Trade |  |  |  |
| Food stores | 1 | 6 | 4 |
| Auto dealers | 8 | 5 | 6 |
| Home furnishing stores | 1 | 5 | 3 |
| Eating and drinking places | 24 | 18 | 21 |
| Miscellaneous retail | 8 | 4 | 6 |
| Other | 6 | 5 | 6 |
| Total | 48 | 43 | 46 |
| Services |  |  |  |
| Hotels | 11 | 11 | 11 |
| Business services | 11 | 11 | 11 |
| Automotive services | 3 | 5 | 4 |
| Other | 17 | 15 | 15 |
| Total | 42 | 42 | 41 |
| Wholesale Trade | 4 | 8 | 6 |
| Manufacturing | 6 | 5 | 6 |
| Construction | 0 | 2 | 1 |

Note: Based on N=360. Categories are derived from business codes (Standard Industrial Classification codes) used by the Bureau of the Census in its Economic Censuses.

The retail trade and services sectors account for 50 percent of all metropolitan area labor forces in both San Diego and Chicago (including jobs at entry level and above, U.S. Department of Labor 1989), but comprise over 80 percent of our sample. Thus, trade and service businesses are overrepresented in our sample in comparison to all jobs. However, our sample may be more representative of entry-level jobs, since much of the growth in low-paying jobs across the nation is occurring in the trade and services sectors (Harrison and Bluestone 1988; Vroman and Vroman 1988).

---

## SIZE OF FIRMS

Testers and site managers had little problem identifying the occupation and type of business of job vacancies sampled. The more difficult task was determining the size of a business. Testers were asked to inquire about or estimate the size of the firms at which they applied for jobs. If the firm was a branch of a larger company (e.g., fast food outlet), testers asked about or estimated the size of the entire company. The initial tester made a direct inquiry at the interview stage, while the comparison tester made an estimate. Tester estimates were reconciled by the site managers in consultation with the testers. In some cases, site managers telephoned employers anonymously to confirm testers' estimates. The results, which should be considered only as rough estimates, are in table 4.4.

During the initial data coding, the size of the firms was divided into four categories as noted in the table. The categories, devised for this study, cover very small and small businesses (up to 10 employees), medium-sized businesses (11-49 employees), and large businesses (50 or more). Medium and large businesses constituted the majority of the employers sampled by the hiring audit. This is to be expected because small businesses generally do not have the resources to advertise for prospective employees in newspapers and probably rely more heavily on informal soliciting methods.

Table 4.4 ESTIMATED SIZE OF COMPANY BY
CITY (percentage of audits)

| Number of Employees | Chicago | San Diego | Total |
|---|---|---|---|
| Less than 4 | 0 | a | a |
| 5 - 10 | 2 | 21 | 12 |
| 11 - 49 | 36 | 49 | 43 |
| 50 or more | 62 | 30 | 45 |

Note: Based on n=354. Size of business was estimated
by testers during site visits.

a. Less than 1%.

There appear to be considerable differences in size of
firms audited at the two study sites. In Chicago, very few
of the businesses sampled (2 percent) had 10 employees or
less, while in San Diego small firms accounted for one-fifth
of the sample (21 percent). Similarly, companies of 50 or
more employees in Chicago made up almost two-thirds
(62 percent) of the sample, while the same figure for San
Diego was only one-third (30 percent).

These differences, like others between the two cities,
may be attributed to their different types of economies
and, to an extent, geographic configurations. San Diego's
economy is smaller and faster growing, and relies heavily
on defense spending and tourism. San Diego is dominated
by small businesses; over 75 percent of all businesses in
that city have less than 15 employees (Marlin 1986).
Chicago's diverse economy dwarfs San Diego's and hosts
heavy concentrations of large-scale financial, retail,
transportation, food processing, and light manufacturing

enterprises. The Loop area alone is the workplace for nearly 600,000 people, and is headquarters to some of the country's largest and oldest companies such as Sears Roebuck and Co.

The geographic layouts of the two cities also reflect the differences in the sizes of businesses sampled. San Diego is mainly a suburban area spread over hundreds of square miles. Chicago is the third largest city in the U.S., with major businesses concentrated within its downtown area. The employers sampled in San Diego were distributed over a range of neighborhoods emanating from its small downtown area. In contrast, the majority of Chicago employers sampled were concentrated in the downtown area of the city. The physical concentration of large businesses in downtown Chicago and the suburban nature of San Diego accounts for much of the proportional differences in sizes of employers between the two cities.

# Chapter Five

# DIFFERENCES IN TREATMENT

This section compares the aggregate differences in treatment for the Anglo and Hispanic testers and addresses the two central research questions.

Before turning to the findings, it is important to define what is meant by "disparate treatment" in this study and to insert a caution about interpreting results. The analysis is based upon how pairs of testers proceed on a comparative basis through the hiring process, which we define as a progression through three stages: 1) application, 2) interview, and 3) job offer. Disparate treatment means differential progress between the two members of a pair during the hiring process (e.g., one obtains an interview and the other does not).

The caution here pertains to the fact that some of the different outcomes may be dependent, and not necessarily the result of disparate treatment. That is, the performance or timing of an individual tester could affect the chances of his partner being offered a job without the employer having treated the partner unfavorably. The impact of dependent outcomes is likely to be greater at the job offer stage than at the application or interview stages, because as testers approach the job offer decision there is a greater likelihood of direct competition (e.g., there is only one job, or the employer only has time to interview one candidate). Shortly, we will address the implications of the dependent outcome effect and show why its impact appears to be minimal.

---

## OVERALL NUMBERS

The testers were generally highly successful in their quest to apply for jobs, obtain interviews, and receive job offers, as indicated in table 5.1 below.  In 93 percent of the 720 individual attempts (360 valid audits multiplied by 2), testers made contact with the employer, filled out an application, and had it accepted by the employer.  The remaining 7 percent are comprised of cases where the employer did not offer an application to one of the paired testers or did not require an application before offering an interview.

In 56 percent of the 720 individual cases, project testers received interviews from prospective employers, and in 30 percent of the cases testers were successful in obtaining offers of employment.  San Diego testers (31 percent) had slightly more success in obtaining job offers than their Chicago counterparts (28 percent), although Chicago testers  were slightly more likely to obtain interviews (58 percent versus 54 percent).

Below is a discussion of the study's findings as they relate to each of the two research questions.

■   RESEARCH QUESTION NO. 1:  Are there differences in how far foreign-looking/ sounding Hispanic job applicants go in the hiring process as compared to those perceived to be U.S. citizens?

Table 5.1  TOTAL NUMBER OF TIMES TESTERS REACHED EACH STAGE
(by city and ethnicity)

| | Chicago[a] | | San Diego[a] | | Total[a] | |
|---|---|---|---|---|---|---|
| | Anglos (n=169) | Hispanics (n=169) | Anglos (n=191) | Hispanics (n=191) | Anglos (n=360) | Hispanics (n=360) |
| Application | 158 (93%) | 149 (88%) | 184 (96%) | 178 (93%) | 342 (95%) | 327 (91%) |
| Interview | 113 (67%) | 82 (49%) | 116 (61%) | 90 (47%) | 229 (64%) | 172 (48%) |
| Job Offer[b] | 59 (42%) | 36 (25%) | 70 (44%) | 49 (31%) | 129 (43%) | 85 (28%) |

a. With the exception of the application outcomes in San Diego, each one-tailed test of the hypothesis that the outcomes are the same for the Anglo and Hispanic tester can be rejected at the 1 percent level.

b. Fifty-eight of the 360 valid audits were terminated before the job offer stage. This accounts for the difference in the totals for the job offer percentages (the base is 302).

Anglo testers on average fared much better than Hispanics in how far they proceeded through the three main hiring stages. *Anglos received 52 percent more job offers than Hispanics.* In Chicago, Anglo testers had 64 percent more job offers than Hispanics, and in San Diego Anglos received 43 percent more job offers. Nearly half the Anglo testers (43 percent) obtained a job offer at the completion of each valid audit. In contrast, less than a third of Hispanic testers (28 percent) received job offers.

The difference in how far each tester group progressed to the interview stage is also considerable. *Anglos received 33 percent more interviews than Hispanics.* The interview outcomes were similar in both cities, with Anglos receiving 37 and 30 percent more interviews than Hispanics in Chicago and San Diego, respectively. Anglo testers reached the interview stage in about two-thirds (64 percent) of the total audits, while Hispanics obtained interviews in less than half (48 percent).

Differences of the magnitude discovered at the job offer and interview stages did not occur at the application stage. Here, 95 percent of Anglo testers and 91 percent of Hispanics filled out applications. By itself, the extent of disparate treatment seems marginal for this stage in the hiring process, although it is still consistent with the pattern of more favorable treatment for Anglos.

Table 5.1 above provides more specific information on how far Anglo and Hispanic testers proceeded in the hiring process. The table reveals a clear pattern. The employers audited in this study seemed willing to accept applications from both testers more or less on an equal basis. However, dramatic differences emerged after applications were filled out, and equality eroded severely by the interview and job offer stages.

One plausible explanation for the difference between the first and later stages of the hiring process is that phone calls and applications are generally received by reception-ist personnel rather than the employer making the inter-view or hiring decision.  As the hiring official(s) get closer to the point of a meaningful decision (job offer or not), there is more opportunity for disparate treatment.  A second plausible explanation involves cost.  It is compara-tively cheap to have a receptionist or clerk accept a completed application, but costly for a manager to inter-view a potential applicant.

■ RESEARCH QUESTION NO. 2:  Are there differences in the numbers of job applications, interviews, and offers obtained by foreign-looking/sounding Hispanic applicants as compared to those appearing to be U.S. citizens?

The response to the previous question provides some of the data required to answer this question, but yields only aggregate numbers.  The response to question no. 2 focuses on how the individual pairs fared by dividing the results by pairs into three outcomes by stage.

- *"Anglo yes, Hispanic no."* This refers to an audit outcome where the Anglo member of the pair proceeds to a stage in the hiring process and the Hispanic does not.

- *"Hispanic yes, Anglo no."* This refers to an outcome where the Hispanic member of the pair proceeds to a stage in the hiring process and the Anglo does not.

- *"Anglo yes, Hispanic yes," and "Anglo no, Hispanic no."* This outcome is a single outcome category where the Anglo and Hispanic members of the pair had the same outcome for the variable in question. This is considered to yield no difference in treatment.

This analytic method enables us to examine the percentages of occurrences where Anglos or Hispanics proceeded further in the hiring process than their partners. By subtracting the percent of audits with "Hispanic yes, Anglo no" from "Anglo yes, Hispanic no," we obtain a measure of "net" disparate treatment. It further permits a determination of the statistical significance of the findings using the normal test of paired differences and an estimate of the intra-cluster correlation coefficient (see Appendices B-3.2 and B-3.3, Johnson Memos). This approach assumes that any unfavorable treatment experienced by Anglos is a random event since Anglos by definition do not experience unfavorable treatment in this country because of national origin. It is also assumed that the amount of random disparate treatment experienced by Anglos is symmetrical to that experienced by Hispanics. The "net" unfavorable treatment of Hispanics, then, is assumed to be the result of systematic disparate treatment, which may be due to discrimination. Some caveats about this approach are discussed in the conclusion.

The outcomes by pairs were compiled for each of the three stages, and were also cumulated across all stages to estimate the overall level of disparate treatment. This overall measure will be discussed in more detail after the differences in the paired outcomes are presented. These estimates are presented in table 5.2. As before, most disparate treatment occurs at the interview and job offer stages. The application stage outcomes in and of themselves do

Table 5.2 PAIRED OUTCOMES BY HIRING STAGE (by audits)

| | Anglo Yes Hispanic No | Hispanic Yes Anglo No | No Difference | Net Difference | Total Sample Size | 95 Percent Confidence Intervals |
|---|---|---|---|---|---|---|
| Application | 6% (21) | 2% (7) | 92% (332) | 4%(14)[a] | 360 | [.01, .07] |
| Interview | 22 (79) | 6 (22) | 72 (259) | 16 (57)[a] | 360 | [.10, .22] |
| Job Offer | 22 (67) | 8 (23) | 70 (211) | 15 (44)[a] | 302[b] | [.09, .21] |
| Overall[c] | 31 (111) | 11 (39) | 58 (210) | 20 (70)[a] | 360 | [.14, .26] |

Note: The numbers in parentheses are the numbers of audits.

a. Each paired difference in treatment is significantly different from zero at the 1 percent level, using a one-tailed test.

b. Fifty-eight of the 360 valid audits were terminated before the job offer stage. This accounts for the difference in the denominator at the job offer stage.

c. The numbers are calculated by counting the first occurrences of disparate treatment. Estimates of net disparate treatment for the 302 valid completed audits are the same as those used for the entire sample.

not indicate major differences.  The net difference (6 percent "Anglo yes, Hispanic no" less 2 percent "Hispanic yes, Anglo no") favoring the Anglo over the Hispanic is only 4 percent.  The net difference increases greatly at the interview stage, where there is a 16 percent differential in the employer decision regarding interviews.  At the job offer stage, the net difference is 15 percent (14.6 percent rounded), again favoring the Anglo.  Not only do the overall numbers (those cumulated across all stages and all pairs) reveal significant differences in treatment as shown in table 5.2, but so do the outcomes for individual pairs. For each pair of testers, the Anglo received more favorable treatment overall than his Hispanic partner.  When examined by the three hiring stages separately, there were only two cases of pairs receiving similar treatment overall, and these only occurred at the application stage.  In all remaining cases for the three stages, the Anglo tester was more successful overall than his Hispanic partner.  Even though the tester pairs averaged only 45 audits each, the overall differences by pair were statistically significant for five of the eight teams.  The differences in treatment by pair are found in table A.6.

## STATISTICAL SIGNIFICANCE

As noted, the precision of these estimates depends on the sample levels of disparate treatment and the size of the intra-cluster correlation coefficient, which reflects the degree to which variation in disparate treatment across pairs dominates the total in variation in treatment across audits.  Other things being equal, the higher the intra-cluster correlation coefficient, the higher the variance and the lower the precision associated with the estimated difference in treatment. The variance of the estimated difference in treatment was calculated for each of the three outcomes using a computer program (developed by GAO statistician Bob Johnson) that relied on well-established formulas from Snecador and Cochrane (1974), and Kish (1965) (see Appendices B-3 and B-5, Johnson Memos).

The intra-cluster correlation coefficients were small for each of the three outcomes; two were negative. In evaluating the adequacy of the sample size prior to implementing the audit, one consideration was the potential for the intra-cluster correlation to be positive. The fact that very small, and even negative, values were found indicates that the pairs were successfully matched. The low values could also be a function of the narrow range of testers employed in the study (i.e., males between 19 and 24 years old with similar educational and work experience).

Tests of whether the differences in treatment were statistically significant were performed for each of the three outcome variables using the net difference in treatment as the numerator and the standard error of the estimate as the denominator (calculated under the null hypothesis of no difference in treatment). In each case the null hypothesis could be rejected at a .005 level using a one-tailed test. Thus, the levels of disparate treatment found in this study are statistically significant. The 95 percent confidence levels presented in table 5.2 indicate the precision associated with each estimate. While the confidence interval is smallest for the application stage, it is large relative to the estimated net difference in treatment.

The research design called for Hispanic and Anglo testers to alternate between who contacted the potential employer first. As a result, Hispanics contacted the employer first in 182 of the 360 audits, while Anglos were first in 178. The order in which the testers initiated contact with employers seems to affect the amount of disparate treatment observed. While initiation of contact was not synonymous with having the first opportunity to be interviewed or offered the job, it is likely that they are highly correlated.

When the Anglo tester initiated the first contact, he received favorable treatment 35 percent of the time and the Hispanic tester received favorable treatment 7 percent of the time. The net difference is 28 percent. In contrast, when the Hispanic tester initiated the first contact, the Anglo tester received favorable treatment 27 percent of the time and the Hispanic received favorable treatment 15 percent of the time, yielding a net difference of 12 percent. Thus, the Hispanic testers seemed to receive much more unfavorable treatment when the employer already knew that there was a similarly qualified Anglo interested in the job. (This finding could imply that in some labor markets, i.e., certain occupations in certain cities where there are relatively few Anglos, one would observe lower levels of disparate treatment.)

These results suggest that the Hispanic testers received less favorable treatment relative to the Anglo tester, whether or not the Hispanic initiated first contact, but that the extent of unfavorable treatment was much higher when the Anglo initiated contact. However, no matter which tester initiated the contact, the differences in treatment are statistically significant at the 5 percent level.

One of the assumptions underlying the variance calculation and tests of significance is that the outcomes for the paired testers are independent (Appendix B-5, Johnson/Stapleton Memo, 10/13/89). To the extent that the outcomes are negatively correlated (i.e., interdependent because perhaps the employer only had one job available), the variance associated with the paired difference in treatment would actually be higher than what has been calculated. To the extent that the paired testers are competing for the same job, the interdependence has the potential to be the greatest at the job offer stage.

Several factors indicate that interdependent outcomes do not significantly affect these findings. First, any tester offered a job quickly turned it down so that his position would remain open for the partner tester. Second, advertisements listing more than one position were over-sampled; fully two-thirds of the firms audited had advertised more than one job. Third, testers obtained job offers in half of the audits, and in 41 percent of these cases, both testers received job offers. Finally, the extent of differential treatment did not seem sensitive to the total number of job openings that firms had listed.

Controlling for ethnicity, both testers had a better chance of obtaining a job offer when more than one job was available. When only one position was advertised, one or both of the testers received an offer 38 percent of the time. When more than one position was advertised, one or both of the testers received an offer 57 percent of the time. However, for a given number of advertised positions, Anglo testers were more likely than Hispanic testers to receive job offers. With one position advertised, Anglos received offers 31 percent of the time, while Hispanics received offers 15 percent of the time, yielding a net difference of 16 percent. With more than one position advertised, the comparable figures were 49 percent and 35 percent, respectively, yielding a net difference of 14 percent in favor of Anglos. The extent of disparate treatment, therefore, appears to be similar regardless of the number of positions advertised.

However, the fact that testers who initiated contact first received favorable treatment 25 percent of the time while the comparison testers received favorable treatment 17 percent of the time suggests that the outcomes may indeed be somewhat related. On the other hand, the high number of audits in which testers received no difference in treatment (92 percent at application, 72 percent at interview, 70 percent at job offer, and 58 percent overall), and the similarity of the findings for audits associated with the number of job openings suggests that the outcomes are not overwhelmingly negatively correlated.

Furthermore, because the t-statistics (which measure how strong the evidence is against the null hypothesis) for the overall measure and for the interview and job offer stages were so high (over 4.5), increases in the variance by a factor of 7 would still lead to rejection of the null hypothesis of no difference in treatment. Therefore, it is unlikely that the conclusions would be substantively changed were the outcomes negatively dependent. Even so, the importance of who initiates first contact should be explored with this dataset in future multivariate analysis, and it should be taken into account in future hiring audit designs.

---

## DISPARATE TREATMENT BY HIRING STAGE

What do these figures on disparate treatment mean? At the interview stage, the Hispanics received unfavorable treatment 22 percent of the time and the Anglos only 6 percent of the time. In our study, therefore, *Hispanic testers experienced three-and-a-half times more unfavorable treatment at the interview stage than the Anglo testers.* When an Anglo tester made his first contact with an employer, there was a 1 in 16 chance that he would receive unfavorable treatment in seeking an interview relative to his similarly qualified Hispanic partner. For the Hispanic seeking an interview, there was a 1 in 4.5 chance of encountering unfavorable treatment.

At the job offer stage, Hispanic testers received unfavorable treatment in 22 percent of the cases, while their Anglo counterparts received unfavorable treatment only 8 percent of the time. *Hispanics, therefore, received three times more unfavorable treatment than Anglos at the job offer stage.* The Hispanic tester faced a 1 in 4.5 chance of unfavorable treatment, while his Anglo partner had only a 1 in 13 chance of unfavorable treatment for job offers (see table 5.2).

---

## OVERALL DISPARATE TREATMENT

The most telling figures on disparate treatment are obtained by aggregating the outcomes at the three hiring stages into an overall measure of disparate treatment. This is achieved by adding together the first occurrences of disparate treatment by stage across all audits. Counting only the first occurrence of disparate treatment avoids double or triple counting incidences of disparate treatment that might have taken place in a single audit. This measurement also shows precisely at which stage the employers first made the differential choices, and it yields a measure of overall disparate treatment. This overall figure provides an indicator of disparate treatment at any point in the hiring process, revealing the probabilities of disparate treatment for Anglos and Hispanics from the moment they make initial contact with the employer until the final outcome is achieved. These differences are shown in table 5.2 above and more graphically in figure 5.1.

Figure 5.1 shows that in the 360 audits carried out by this study, Anglos received favorable treatment relative to their Hispanic partners in 111 audits (or 31 percent of the cases). Hispanics received favorable treatment relative to their Anglo partners in 39 cases, or 10 percent of the time. Thus, assuming that they are competing with Anglo applicants, young Hispanic men who are "foreign-looking/sounding" in San Diego and Chicago can expect to encounter disparate treatment 3 times for every 10 jobs for which they apply through the newspaper. In contrast, Anglos can expect to encounter unfavorable treatment in only 1 of every 10 jobs they seek where there are also Hispanic applicants.

*Overall, the results from our sample show that Hispanic men are three times as likely to encounter unfavorable treatment when applying for jobs as similarly qualified Anglos.*

If we "net out" unfavorable treatment for each group of pairs (31 percent minus 11 percent), there remains a 20 percent difference in disparate treatment for Hispanic testers. *This means that our Hispanic testers faced net disparate treatment in one of every five jobs sought.* Statistical tests reveal that this level of disparate treatment is not likely to have occurred by chance. The 95 percent confidence interval for the true difference in treatment (or net level of unfavorable treatment) is .14 to .26.

---

## COMPARISON TO OTHER STUDIES

Little comparable work has been conducted on disparate treatment between Hispanics and Anglos. Major national studies have been completed on disparate treatment in the housing market between blacks and whites, and two small

Figure 5.1 OVERALL DISPARATE TREATMENT
First Occurrence by Stage

| Application | | Interview | | Job Offer | |
|---|---|---|---|---|---|
| Anglo completes, Hispanic does not | 21 | Anglo receives, Hispanic does not | 63 | Anglo receives, Hispanic does not | 27 |
| Hispanic completes, Anglo does not | 7 | Hispanic receives, Anglo does not | 18 | Hispanic receives, Anglo does not | 14 |

+ +

| Hiring Process Outcome | Cumulative Differences | Percent Differences |
|---|---|---|
| Anglo Favored | 111 | 31% |
| Hispanic Favored | 39 | 11% |

Note: Only the first occurrence of disparate treatment is included. Total number of audits = 360.

housing audits have been undertaken for Hispanics and Anglos. A recently completed "National Housing Discrimination Study" conducted by HUD and The Urban Institute should yield a wealth of information on disparate treatment between Hispanics and Anglos in the housing market (results expected in August 1990).

Findings from the studies on disparate treatment completed to date reveal trends similar to those found in this hiring audit. However, these audits are only broadly comparable because 1) they pertain to housing, not employment, 2) the HUD national housing study examined disparate treatment of blacks, not Hispanics, and 3) the sample sizes for the Hispanic housing audits were small and only marginally statistically significant.

HUD's 1977 Housing Market Practices Survey showed net differences in treatment between Black and White testers of 27 percent for apartments and 15 percent for home sales, favoring White testers. At the time, HUD labeled these findings as proof of gross levels of discrimination against blacks in the housing market (Wienk et al. 1979).

A 1978 HUD audit of the rental market in Dallas showed a 16 percent difference in overall treatment between "light-skinned" Hispanics and Anglos (Hakken 1979), although the findings were not statistically significant. In 1982 researchers at the University of Colorado conducted a housing audit in Denver that revealed statistically significant differences in treatment between whites and Hispanics of 15 and 16 percent for two key rental indicators (James et al. 1984).

## DISPARATE TREATMENT BY CITIES, OCCUPATIONS AND BUSINESSES

The figures on disparate outcomes can be broken down by city, occupation, and business. Specific data on these outcomes can be found in appendix A. While cross tabular analyses point out some interesting patterns, it should be kept in mind that multivariate analysis is required to sort out separate effects of the individual variables on disparate treatment. *There were notable differences in the extent of disparate treatment found in Chicago and San Diego, but the findings are statistically significant in both locations.*

Hispanic testers encountered greater disparate treatment in Chicago. The overall figures show that Hispanic testers received unfavorable treatment in 33 percent of the Chicago audits, while the figure for Anglos was only 8 percent (see table A.1). The net difference of 25 percent in disparate treatment unfavorable to Hispanics contrasts with a net difference of 16 percent in San Diego (table A.2). Both figures are statistically significant from zero at the 5 percent level and show that Hispanic job seekers can expect a measure of disparate treatment in both cities. While it appears that the extent of disparate treatment is higher in Chicago than in San Diego, the hypothesis that the two estimates were equal could not be rejected at the 5 percent level.

A possible hypothesis for explaining the difference is that, unlike Chicago, San Diego is historically, culturally, and geographically tied to the Mexican border, and therefore is more accepting of Hispanics. Hispanics, especially Mexicans, have coexisted with Anglos in the San Diego area for 150 years and are not necessarily seen as "outsiders." Chicago, on the other hand, is ethnically diverse and contains discernible ethnic neighborhoods. Hispanic migration to Chicago began after the turn of the century, was repressed in the 1930s, and did not pick up again until after World War II. Lacking a long cultural history with Hispanics, Chicago's majority citizens may be less accepting than their counterparts in San Diego.

Another plausible explanation for the differences in treatment may involve differences in unemployment rates between the two cities. As noted above, these differences are substantial and could possibly influence employer behavior. The "loose" labor market in Chicago may provide employers with a greater latitude to treat Hispanics unfavorably because the employers know they have other choices. Conversely, employers in San Diego face a "tight" labor market and so may be more open to applicants of any ethnicity.

Overall differences in treatment by occupation appear to vary little from the overall average, with the exception of the "management," and "service, other" categories (table A.3). Hispanic testers fared the best with "service, other" occupational jobs, for which the net negative disparate treatment was not significantly different from 0 at the 5 percent level. Management and office occupations posed a greater barrier for the Hispanic testers. They experienced net unfavorable treatment in 32 and 26 percent of the audits for management and office positions, respectively. These outcomes could be linked to stereotypes held by employers about appropriate jobs for ethnic applicants.

Examining overall differences by type of business is useful because it can point out the most potentially productive sectors in which to pursue measures to counter disparate treatment in job hiring. The largest measure of disparate treatment occurs in the manufacturing and construction businesses sampled. (See table A.4.) The net difference in treatment found here is 33 percent, compared to 20 percent across all business types (we did not test whether the 33 percent figure was different from the mean). The two largest types of businesses sampled--services (15 percent difference) and retail trade (23 percent difference)--revealed differences close to the average. Although the combined figure for manufacturing and construction was statistically significant from zero, the number of cases was low (n=24), as was the precision of the estimate. These numbers and percent differences suggest that future audits seeking to identify businesses most likely to treat Hispanics unfavorably may wish to oversample manufacturing and construction businesses to increase the precision of the estimates.

---

## QUALITATIVE DIFFERENCES

The differences in treatment presented thus far pertain to comparisons of how Anglo and Hispanic testers fared along three objective outcomes (applications, interviews, and job offers). Although the results of these analyses are clear, they do not by any means tell the whole story of the disparate treatment observed in the job market.

In this study testers sometimes reached the same stage in the hiring process, but would still experience differential treatment from the prospective employer. These instances often occurred at the interview stage, and involved the amount of information given to each tester, the stated career potential of the job, and the exact type of job deemed "suitable" for the applicant by the employer. Much of information on this more subtle type of disparate treatment is not easily quantifiable. It was identified through open-ended tester comments at the end of the survey and collected anecdotally by the site managers during the daily debriefings.

In coding qualitative differences based on tester comments, only those in which there was a clear example of differential treatment (e.g., Anglo told he would advance in two months to higher paying job and Hispanic not given this information, Anglo offered waiter job and Hispanic offered busboy job, etc.) were noted. Not included as a qualitative difference were the courtesy and demeanor of the employer toward the testers, which varied greatly in some cases. Based upon tester comments, in 14 audits employers treated the Anglo more favorably than the Hispanic. In two cases, employers treated Hispanics more favorably than Anglos at the same stage. If these differences could be added to the differences in overall treatment above, the net difference in treatment would be 23 percent in favor of Anglos. This is slightly larger than the 20 percent found in figure 5.1.

Typical of the qualitative differences is the following example. The Hispanic tester fills out an application and is given a short interview about the busboy job for which he is applying. The basics of the job and pay are covered by the interviewer. The Anglo tester fills out the application and is given a longer interview, during which he is told that if he works well he can quickly move up to higher paying bartender or even host jobs within a short time. He is introduced to several other employees. This is a case where both testers reached the interview stage but preferential treatment clearly was given to the Anglo.

Another indicator for these qualitative, less precise differences is the length of time given to each tester for an interview. The assumption here is that employers treat applicants more favorably if they spend more time with them during the interview. It is conceivable the opposite

Table 5.3   MEAN LENGTH OF INTERVIEW BY OUTCOME
(in minutes)

|  | Chicago | | San Diego | |
|---|---|---|---|---|
|  | Anglo | Hispanics | Anglo | Hispanics |
| Job Offered | 22.7 | 17.1 | 16.1 | 12.1 |
| No Job Offered | 15.6 | 12.7 | 10.9 | 10.6 |

Note: Based on N=401.

could be true. Marked differences were found in the amount of time employers would devote to each of the paired testers at the interview stage. The average length of interview time for those who received job offers compared to those who did not are presented in table 5.3.

For testers receiving job offers, employers spent one-third more time interviewing Anglos than Hispanics in both cities. For testers interviewed but not offered jobs, employers spent one-fifth more time with Anglos in Chicago and an equal amount of time with both ethnic groups in San Diego. These differences could have occurred because the employer felt that he/she needed to be more assured about the Anglo applicants, or because he/she had more interest in interviewing Anglos.

This may not be surprising in view of the fact that in this hiring audit, 87 percent of the interviewers in Chicago and 82 percent of the interviewers in San Diego were identified by the testers as "white." Males constituted two-thirds of the white interviewers. Only 9 percent of the interviewers were either Hispanic (5 percent) or Black (4 percent). Distributions of interviewer ethnicities were similar for both cities (table A.17).

Measures of qualitative differences such as those above could be incorporated into further hiring audits and added to the aggregate numbers.

# Chapter Six

## CONCLUSIONS

This study began with the objective of measuring disparate treatment in the job market for young Hispanic job seekers. To obtain these measurements, the study audited randomly selected employers in two major cities using Hispanic and Anglo testers similarly qualified in key job-related characteristics. The study utilized a variety of techniques to control carefully the research and to collect accurate information. A total of 360 audits were successfully carried out, producing a wealth of statistically significant findings.

The results show that foreign-looking and -sounding Hispanics in San Diego and Chicago face considerable barriers compared to their Anglo counterparts in obtaining interviews and offers of employment for low-skilled, entry-level jobs. Specifically,

- Hispanic testers received unfavorable treatment from 3 of every 10 employers;

- Hispanic testers were three times more likely to encounter unfavorable treatment when applying for jobs than similarly qualified Anglos;

- Anglos received 33 percent more interviews than Hispanics; and

- Anglos received 52 percent more job offers than Hispanics.

Anglo testers also experienced disparate treatment, but at much lower levels than their Hispanic counterparts. Anglos received unfavorable treatment in 1 in 10 of the audits.

---

## *DISPARATE TREATMENT AND DISCRIMINATION: DISCUSSION*

The key question underlying the findings on disparate treatment is: *What has the hiring audit detected and how do we explain disparate treatment?*

The study found dramatic differences in the employment outcomes of matched Anglo/Hispanic pairs. Hispanic testers received unfavorable treatment in 31 percent of the audits while the Anglo testers received unfavorable treatment in only 11 percent of the audits. However, several caveats should be noted when interpreting these findings.

First, while the recruitment, training, and matching processes were explicitly designed to achieve pairings closely matched in employment-relevant characteristics, it is possible that Hispanics had other attributes that made them less desirable job candidates. As discussed above, to make the Hispanic and Anglo testers similarly qualified job candidates, controls were introduced for the quantity and quality of educational background, work experience, age, citizenship, physical condition, availability, fluency in English, dress, height, weight, salary desired, demeanor, and so on. Other characteristics relevant to employer decisions, if correlated with the ethnicity of the tester, could bias the finding on disparate treatment related to ethnicity in either direction. Such characteristics might include the firmness of voice or strength of handshake, or more likely, attitudinal traits not modified during the training sessions. While this possible source of bias cannot be dismissed, it is probably unlikely that these types of factors could lead to the large amounts of disparate treatment found in this study. In addition, it was not possible to control for the number and characteristics of other "real" job seekers whose job applications might have affected employers' decisions regarding the tester applicants. But again, it is difficult to understand how or why these factors would lead to this study's significant amount of disparate treatment.

Second, these audits were carried out in only two cities by young male testers, half of whom were identifiably Hispanic, and the audits covered only a subset of jobs and employers in each city. The amount of disparate treatment found here may not be representative of that found in other cities or for other Hispanic job seekers. Depending on the group used as testers, levels of disparate treatment could be lower or higher. These other groups of job seekers could include older, female, more accented, or less ethnic-appearing Hispanics.

It should be noted, however, that some characteristics of the cities and jobs suggest the results could have applicability beyond the two cities studied. As observed earlier, the two cities selected for the audit have a measure of regional representativeness. The types of jobs sampled underrepresent certain occupations such as technical and manufacturing, since about three-quarters of the jobs sampled were in the sales and services occupational categories. However, the majority of these occupations are among the fastest growing or will provide the largest number of new jobs in the 1990s. For example, the Census Bureau estimates that between 1986 and 2000 the U.S. will have added 1.2 million retail sales jobs and one-half million *each* cashiers, guards, waitpersons, and food counter persons (U.S. Bureau of the Census 1989). While the sample is drawn from only a subset of employers in two cities, it nevertheless represents a large portion of the job market facing young Hispanics in the decade of the 1990s.

Eleven percent of the employers in the audit are recognizable national companies with multiple locations spread across the U.S. They include some of the largest hotel chains, retail stores, financial institutions, restaurants, and service agencies in the nation. Together, these firms have more than a million employees; several have more than 100,000 employees (Standard and Poor 1988). While one cannot generalize about an entire company based on experiences in a single location, it is likely that overall corporate mentality, training programs, company policies, and management leadership combine to influence the behavior of employees making hiring decisions in any one location.

Finally, disparate treatment can result from systematic behavior such as discrimination, or from random events such as an employer's bad mood. It is possible that disparate treatment is entirely related to systematic behavior, random behavior, or some combination of both. The method used for this study subtracts unfavorable treatment of Anglos from unfavorable treatment of Hispanics to arrive at "net disparate treatment." The assumption underlying this method is that random events are cancelled out by the subtraction so that the residual accounts for systematic behavior. This approach assumes that random unfavorable treatment is symmetrical for

Anglo and Hispanic outcomes. The U.S. Department of Housing and Urban Development used the same methodology in its 1977 national housing audit (Wienk et al. 1979).

Some researchers believe this approach is conservative, resulting in a lower bound estimate of the amount of disparate treatment accounted for by systematic behavior. Yinger (1988), for example, would argue that both Anglo and Hispanic unfavorable treatment contain some random and some systematic elements, and that it is problematic to distinguish the amount of each. (This, in any event, could not be done with the methodology used in this study.) Like the 1977 housing audit, this audit assumes that any favorable treatment of minorities is random and that it is a good measure of the probable amount of random favorable treatment received by Anglos. Yinger, on the other hand, argues that it is logical that random treatment of both ethnic groups is not symmetrical. According to this thinking, Hispanics could be favored because the employer thought a job was more "appropriate" for a Hispanic. (This in fact happened in this audit when a Hispanic received a busboy job offer and his Anglo counterpart was told to come back in two weeks to interview for the bartender job.) Counting such treatment as random, as was done in this study, can lead to an underestimation of the level of systematic disparate treatment.

Sophisticated discrete choice models are being developed in the housing audit field to disentangle random and systematic components. Future analysis of the data from this audit to make use of such models should shed light on the issue.

## FINAL WORDS

These caveats do not change the fact that about one-third of the time (31 percent), similarly qualified Hispanic job seekers in this study were treated less favorably than young Anglo job seekers.

The findings of this study indicate that discrimination may be one explanation for the higher unemployment rates observed among Hispanics. Hispanic job seekers who encounter difficulties obtaining jobs may become discouraged and drop out of the labor force or may spend a longer time unemployed. These findings suggest that reducing unemployment and poverty among the Hispanic population may be more difficult than previously imagined. More attention is warranted to determine how employment barriers facing Hispanic and other minorities can be lessened and whether the hiring audit methodology can be used as a tool for monitoring (or possibly enforcing) equal opportunity laws.

In sum, this study documents sizeable disparities in the treatment of Hispanic and Anglo testers in Chicago and San Diego. We believe that a significant portion of this disparate treatment is the result of discrimination.

# APPENDICES

*Appendix A*

# ADDITIONAL TABLES

Table A.1  OVERALL DISPARATE TREATMENT FOR CHICAGO
First Occurrence by Stage

| Application | | Interview | | Job Offer |
|---|---|---|---|---|
| Anglo completes; Hispanic does not | 10 | Anglo receives; Hispanic does not | 28 | Anglo receives; Hispanic does not | 18 |
| Hispanic completes; Anglo does not | 2 | Hispanic receives; Anglo does not | 4 | Hispanic receives; Anglo does not | 8 |

| Hiring Process Outcome | Cumulative Differences | Percent Differences* |
|---|---|---|
| Anglo Favored | 56 | 33% |
| Hispanic Favored | 14 | 8% |

Note:  Only the first occurrence of disparate treatment is included.  Total number of audits = 169.

* These differences were significantly different from each other at the 5 percent level using a one-tailed test.

Table A.2  OVERALL DISPARATE TREATMENT FOR SAN DIEGO
First Occurrence by Stage

| **Application** | | **Interview** | | **Job Offer** | |
|---|---|---|---|---|---|
| Anglo completes; Hispanic does not | 11 | Anglo receives; Hispanic does not | 35 | Anglo receives; Hispanic does not | 9 |
| Hispanic completes; Anglo does not | 5 | Hispanic receives; Anglo does not | 14 | Hispanic receives; Anglo does not | 6 |

| Hiring Process Outcome | Cumulative Differences | Percent Differences * |
|---|---|---|
| Anglo Favored | 55 | 29% |
| Hispanic Favored | 25 | 13% |

Note: Only the first occurrence of disparate treatment is included. Total number of audits = 191.

* These differences were significantly different from each other at the 5 percent level using a one-tailed test.

Table A.3  OVERALL DIFFERENCES IN TREATMENT BY OCCUPATION (first occurrence by stage)

| | Application | | Interview | | Job Offer | | Overall | | % Differ- |
| | Anglo Favored | Hispanic Favored | Anglo Favored | Hispanic Favored | Anglo Favored | Hispanic Favored | Anglo Favored | Hispanic Favored | ence* |
|---|---|---|---|---|---|---|---|---|---|
| Sales (n=58) | 3 | 1 | 11 | 2 | 5 | 2 | 19 | 5 | 24 |
| Services | | | | | | | | | |
| Hotel (n=37) | 1 | 0 | 10 | 3 | 1 | 0 | 12 | 3 | 24 |
| Other (n=81) | 3 | 4 | 13 | 7 | 5 | 4 | 21 | 15 | 7* |
| Restaurant (n=81) | 3 | 0 | 19 | 3 | 8 | 7 | 30 | 10 | 25 |
| Office (n=36) | 5 | 2 | 4 | 0 | 1 | 0 | 10 | 2 | 22 |
| Management (n=16) | 4 | 0 | 1 | 1 | 1 | 0 | 6 | 1 | 31 |
| Technical (n=18) | 2 | 0 | 1 | 2 | 2 | 0 | 5 | 2 | 17 |
| General Labor (n=33) | 0 | 0 | 4 | 0 | 4 | 1 | 8 | 1 | 21 |
| Total | 21 | 7 | 63 | 18 | 27 | 14 | 111 | 39 | 20 |

(n=360 for application and interview, n=302 for job offer.)

Note:  The numbers are calculated by counting only the first occurrence of disparate treatment.

*These percent differences were not significantly different from zero at a significance level of 5 percent, based on a one-tailed test.

Table A.4   OVERALL DIFFERENCES IN TREATMENT BY TYPE OF BUSINESS (first occurrence by stage)

| | Application | | Interview | | Job Offer | | Overall | | % Differ-ence* |
|---|---|---|---|---|---|---|---|---|---|
| | Anglo Favored | Hispanic Favored | Anglo Favored | Hispanic Favored | Anglo Favored | Hispanic Favored | Anglo Favored | Hispanic Favored | |
| Construction (n=4) | 0 | 0 | 0 | 0 | 1 | 0 | 1 | 0 | 25* |
| Manufacturing (n=20) | 2 | 0 | 3 | 0 | 2 | 0 | 7 | 0 | 35 |
| Retail (n=163) | 9 | 3 | 34 | 7 | 15 | 10 | 58 | 20 | 23 |
| Service (n=150) | 10 | 3 | 20 | 8 | 7 | 3 | 37 | 14 | 15 |
| Wholesale (n=23) | 0 | 1 | 6 | 3 | 2 | 1 | 8 | 5 | 13 |
| Total | 21 | 7 | 63 | 18 | 27 | 14 | 111 | 39 | 20 |

(n=360 for application and interview, n=302 for job offer.)

Note:  The numbers are calculated by counting only the first occurrence of disparate treatment.

*These percent differences were not significantly different from zero at a significance level of 5 percent, based on a one-tailed test.

Table A.5    OVERALL DIFFERENCES IN TREATMENT BY SIZE OF BUSINESS AND FIRST OCCURRENCE BY STAGE

| | Application | | Interview | | Job Offer | | Overall | | % |
|---|---|---|---|---|---|---|---|---|---|
| | Anglo Favored | Hispanic Favored | Anglo Favored | Hispanic Favored | Anglo Favored | Hispanic Favored | Anglo Favored | Hispanic Favored | Differ-ence* |
| Small 1-10 employees (n=44) | 3 | 1 | 8 | 1 | 4 | 3 | 15 | 5 | 23 |
| Medium 11-49 employees (n=151) | 7 | 5 | 25 | 11 | 10 | 4 | 42 | 20 | 15 |
| Large 50+ employees (n=159) | 11 | 1 | 30 | 6 | 13 | 7 | 54 | 14 | 25 |
| Total (n=354) | 21 | 7 | 63 | 18 | 27 | 14 | 111 | 39 | 20 |

(n=354 for application and interview, n=302 for job offer.)

Note: The numbers are calculated by counting only the first occurrence of disparate treatment.

*These percent differences were not significantly different from zero at a significance level of 5 percent, based on a one-tailed test.

Table A.6    DIFFERENCES IN TREATMENT BY HIRING STAGE AND BY PAIR AND OVERALL DIFFERENCES BY PAIR

| | Application | | Interview | | Job Offer | | Overall | | |
|---|---|---|---|---|---|---|---|---|---|
| | Anglo Favored | Hispanic Favored | Anglo Favored | Hispanic Favored | Anglo Favored | Hispanic Favored | Anglo Favored | Hispanic Favored | % Difference |
| Pair 1 (n=49) | 2 | 0 | 14 | 4 | 6 | 4 | 14 | 6 | 16 |
| Pair 2 (n=42) | 4 | 2 | 7 | 5 | 9 | 2 | 13 | 7 | 14* |
| Pair 3 (n=54) | 3 | 1 | 12 | 4 | 11 | 2 | 15 | 5 | 18 |
| Pair 4 (n=46) | 2 | 2 | 11 | 4 | 8 | 5 | 13 | 7 | 13* |
| Pair 5 (n=40) | 4 | 0 | 9 | 1 | 7 | 1 | 15 | 1 | 35 |
| Pair 6 (n=37) | 3 | 1 | 9 | 2 | 9 | 2 | 15 | 3 | 32 |
| Pair 7 (n=48) | 1 | 1 | 3 | 1 | 7 | 3 | 8 | 4 | 8* |
| Pair 8 (n=44) | 2 | 0 | 14 | 1 | 10 | 4 | 18 | 6 | 27 |
| Total | 21 | 7 | 79 | 22 | 67 | 23 | 111 | 39 | 20 |

(n=360 for application and interview, n=302 for job offer.)

Note: The overall numbers are not the sums of the previous columns because they do not double or triple count the occurrences of disparate treatment.

*These percent differences were not significantly different from zero at a significance level of 5 percent, based on a one-tailed test.

Table A.7     APPLICATION DIFFERENCES BY
              OCCUPATION (for audit pairs)

|            | Anglo Favored | | Hispanic Favored | | No Difference | |
|------------|---|--------|---|-------|-----|--------|
| Sales      | 3 | (5%)   | 1 | (2%)  | 54  | (73%)  |
| Services   |   |        |   |       |     |        |
| Hotel      | 1 | (3%)   | 0 | (0%)  | 37  | (97%)  |
| Other      | 3 | (4%)   | 4 | (5%)  | 73  | (91%)  |
| Restaurant | 3 | (4%)   | 0 | (0%)  | 78  | (96%)  |
| Office     | 5 | (17%)  | 2 | (6%)  | 29  | (77%)  |
| Management | 4 | (25%)  | 0 | (0%)  | 12  | (75%)  |
| Technical  | 2 | (11%)  | 0 | (0%)  | 16  | (98%)  |
| Labor      | 0 | (0%)   | 0 | (0%)  | 33  | (100%) |
| Total      | 21| (6%)   | 7 | (2%)  | 332 | (92%)  |

(n=360)

Note: This table was prepared for descriptive purposes. No hypothesis test was done for these variables.

Table A.8    INTERVIEW DIFFERENCES BY OCCUPATION
(for audit pairs)

| | Anglo Favored | | Hispanic Favored | | No Difference | |
|---|---|---|---|---|---|---|
| Sales | 12 | (21%) | 3 | (5%) | 43 | (75%) |
| Services | | | | | | |
| Hotel | 11 | (30%) | 3 | (8%) | 23 | (62%) |
| Other | 15 | (18%) | 8 | (10%) | 58 | (72%) |
| Restaurant | 21 | (26%) | 3 | (4%) | 57 | (70%) |
| Office | 10 | (28%) | 2 | (8%) | 24 | (64%) |
| Management | 3 | (19%) | 1 | (6%) | 12 | (75%) |
| Technical | 3 | (17%) | 2 | (11%) | 13 | (72%) |
| Labor | 4 | (12%) | 0 | (0%) | 29 | (88%) |
| Total | 79 | (22%) | 22 | (6%) | 259 | (72%) |

(n=360)

Note: This table was prepared for descriptive purposes. No hypothesis test was done for these variables.

Table A.9 JOB OFFER DIFFERENCES BY OCCUPATION[a]
(for audit pairs)

| | Anglo Favored | | Hispanic Favored | | No Difference | |
|---|---|---|---|---|---|---|
| Sales | 11 | (22%) | 2 | (4%) | 37 | (74%) |
| Services | | | | | | |
| Hotel | 8 | (27%) | 1 | (3%) | 21 | (70%) |
| Other | 12 | (17%) | 8 | (11%) | 50 | (72%) |
| Restaurant | 18 | (27%) | 8 | (12%) | 41 | (61%) |
| Office | 6 | (21%) | 0 | (0%) | 23 | (79%) |
| Management | 1 | (7%) | 1 | (7%) | 12 | (86%) |
| Technical | 4 | (25%) | 2 | (12%) | 10 | (63%) |
| Labor | 7 | (27%) | 1 | (4%) | 18 | (69%) |
| Total | 67 | (22%) | 23 | (8%) | 212 | (70%) |

(n=302)

Note: This table was prepared for descriptive purposes. No hypothesis test was done for these variables.

a. Data are for completed audits only. A completed audit is defined as a valid audit where the employer had at least two full weeks to make a job offer decision for at least one tester.

Table A.10    APPLICATION DIFFERENCES BY TYPE OF
BUSINESS (for audit pairs)

|  | Anglo Favored | | Hispanic Favored | | No Difference | |
|---|---|---|---|---|---|---|
| Construction | 0 | (0%) | 0 | (0%) | 4 | (100%) |
| Manufacturing | 2 | (10%) | 0 | (0%) | 18 | (90%) |
| Retail | 8 | (6%) | 3 | (2%) | 152 | (92%) |
| Service | 11 | (7%) | 3 | (2%) | 136 | (91%) |
| Wholesale | 0 | (0%) | 1 | (4%) | 22 | (96%) |
| Total | 21 | (6%) | 7 | (2%) | 332 | (92%) |

(n=360)

Note: This table was prepared for descriptive purposes. No hypothesis test was done for these variables.

Table A.11   INTERVIEW DIFFERENCES BY TYPE OF
             BUSINESS (for audit pairs)

|              | Anglo Favored | | Hispanic Favored | | No Difference | |
|--------------|------|--------|------|--------|------|---------|
| Construction | 0  | (0%)  | 0  | (0%)  | 4   | (100%) |
| Manufacturing| 5  | (25%) | 0  | (0%)  | 15  | (75%)  |
| Retail       | 39 | (24%) | 8  | (5%)  | 116 | (71%)  |
| Service      | 29 | (19%) | 10 | (7%)  | 111 | (74%)  |
| Wholesale    | 6  | (26%) | 4  | (17%) | 13  | (57%)  |
| Total        | 79 | (22%) | 22 | (7%)  | 259 | (72%)  |

(n=360)

Note: This table was prepared for descriptive purposes.  No hypothesis
test was done for these variables.

Table A.12   JOB OFFER DIFFERENCES BY TYPE OF
             BUSINESS (for audit pairs)

|  | Anglo Favored | | Hispanic Favored | | No Difference | |
|---|---|---|---|---|---|---|
| Construction | 1 | (25%) | 0 | (0%) | 3 | (75%) |
| Manufacturing | 5 | (33%) | 0 | (0%) | 10 | (67%) |
| Retail | 34 | (25%) | 13 | (10%) | 89 | (65%) |
| Service | 23 | (18%) | 6 | (5%) | 99 | (77%) |
| Wholesale | 4 | (21%) | 4 | (21%) | 11 | (58%) |
| Total | 67 | (22%) | 23 | (8%) | 212 | (70%) |

(n=302)

Note: This table was prepared for descriptive purposes. No hypothesis test was done for these variables.

Table A.13    APPLICATION DIFFERENCES BY SIZE OF
             BUSINESS (for audit pairs)

|  | Anglo Favored | | Hispanic Favored | | No Difference | |
|---|---|---|---|---|---|---|
| Small (1-10 employees) | 3 | (7%) | 1 | (2%) | 40 | (91%) |
| Medium (11-49 employees) | 7 | (13%) | 5 | (9%) | 39 | (78%) |
| Large (50+ employees) | 11 | (7%) | 1 | (1%) | 153 | (92%) |
| Total | 21 | (6%) | 7 | (2%) | 332 | (92%) |

(n=360)

Note:  This table was prepared for descriptive purposes.  No hypothesis
test was done for these variables.

Table A.14    INTERVIEW DIFFERENCES BY SIZE OF
             BUSINESS (for audit pairs)

|  | Anglo Favored | | Hispanic Favored | | No Difference | |
|---|---|---|---|---|---|---|
| Small (1-10 employees) | 10 | (23%) | 1 | (2%) | 33 | (74%) |
| Medium (11-49 employees) | 31 | (21%) | 14 | (9%) | 106 | (70%) |
| Large (50+ employees) | 38 | (23%) | 7 | (4%) | 120 | (73%) |
| Total | 79 | (22%) | 22 | (6%) | 331 | (72%) |

(n=360)

Note: This table was prepared for descriptive purposes. No hypothesis test was done for these variables.

Table A.15    JOB OFFER DIFFERENCES BY SIZE OF
             BUSINESS[a] (for audit pairs)

|  | Anglo Favored | | Hispanic Favored | | No Difference | |
| --- | --- | --- | --- | --- | --- | --- |
| Small (5-10 employees) | 10 | (27%) | 3 | (8%) | 24 | (65%) |
| Medium (11-49 employees) | 22 | (17%) | 9 | (7%) | 97 | (76%) |
| Large (50+ employees) | 35 | (26%) | 11 | (8%) | 88 | (66%) |
| Total | 67 | (22%) | 23 | (8%) | 209 | (70%) |

(n=299)

Note: This table was prepared for descriptive purposes. No hypothesis test was done for these variables.

Table A.16    CHARACTERISTICS OF INTERVIEWERS BY
                         CITY

|  | Chicago (percent) | San Diego (percent) | Total (percent) |
|---|---|---|---|
| **Ethnicity of Interviewer** | | | |
| White | 87 | 82 | 83 |
| Black | 5 | 5 | 4 |
| Hispanic | 4 | 5 | 5 |
| Asian | 2 | 3 | 3 |
| Unknown | 2 | 7 | 5 |
| **Sex of Interviewer** | | | |
| Male | 64 | 65 | 65 |
| Female | 36 | 35 | 35 |

(n=401)

Table A.17   NUMBER OF VALID AUDITS BY PAIRS

| | |
|---|---:|
| San Diego | |
| Pair 1 | 49 |
| Pair 2 | 42 |
| Pair 3 | 54 |
| Pair 4 | 46 |
| Chicago | |
| Pair 5 | 40 |
| Pair 6 | 37 |
| Pair 7 | 48 |
| Pair 8 | 44 |
| Total | |
| 8 Pairs | 360 |

Table A.18 COMPLETED STAGES BY ETHNICITY FOR BOTH CITIES

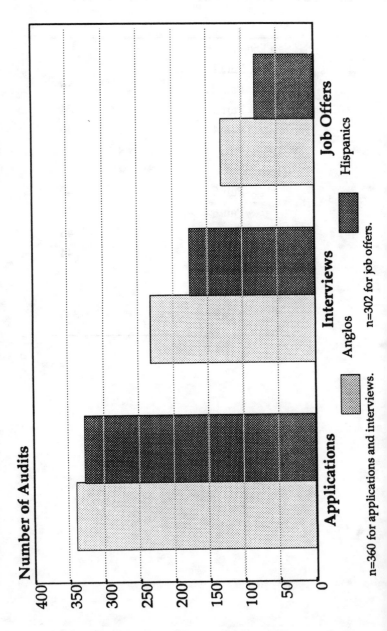

n=360 for applications and interviews.

n=302 for job offers.

Table A.19     DIFFERENCES IN OUTCOMES BY ORDER OF TESTERS

|  | Number of Audits | Anglo Favored | Hispanic Favored | Net Difference |
|---|---|---|---|---|
| Anglo Initiates | 178 | 62 (35%) | 12 (7%) | 50 (28%)[*] |
|   95% confidence | | | | |
|   interval | | | | (.20, .36) |
| Hispanic Initiates | 182 | 49 (27%) | 27 (15%) | 21 (12%)[*] |
|   95% confidence | | | | |
|   interval | | | | (.03, .21) |

(n=360)

Note: The term "favored" means that one tester was more successful at any particular stage (application, interview, job offer) than his partner. For example, the Anglo tester was invited for an interview and the Hispanic tester was not.

[*] These differences were significant at the 5% level using a one-tailed test.

## *Appendix B*[*]

## RESEARCH DESIGN AND TESTER TRAINING

B-1   Site Selection

B-2   Research Memos--Research Design

B-3   Research Memos--Sample

B-4   Research Memos--Testers

B-5   Research Memos--Data Analysis

B-6   Tester Selection Criteria

B-7   Probability Table

B-8   Examples of Entry Level, Low-Skilled Occupations

B-9   Occupations Excluded from Sample

B-10  Simulated Tester Biographies

B-11  Audit Forms

B-12  Tester Training Manual

[*] As noted in the Preface, Appendix B is not contained in this report. It does appear in the full version of this study, which is available through The Urban Institute's Publications Office under the title *Differential Treatment Between Hispanic and Anglo Jobseekers: A Study of Hiring Practices in Two Cities*, Cross et al., November 1989.

# BIBLIOGRAPHY

Abraham, Katharine G. 1987. "Help-Wanted Advertising, Job Vacancies, and Unemployment." *Brookings Papers on Economic Activities*, 1:1987, Washington, D.C.: Brookings Institution.

Bendick, Marc, Jr. 1989. "Auditing Race Discrimination in Hiring: An Initial Research Design" (draft). Washington, D.C.: Bendick and Egan Economic Consultants, Inc.

Broder, David S. 1989. "The Decade of Patchy Prosperity." *The Washington Post* (Sunday, Dec. 10), Washington, D.C.

Cain, Glen G. 1986. "The Economic Analysis of Labor Market Discrimination: A Survey." In *Handbook of Labor Economics*, vol. 1, edited by O. Ashenfelter and R. Layard. New York: Elsevier Science Publishers BV.

Calhoun, Charles A. 1988. "Statistical Issues Of Paired Comparisons." Washington, D.C.: Urban Institute.

Cross, Harry. 1989. "Hiring Audit Research Design." Washington, D.C.: Urban Institute.

Cross, Harry, Genevieve Kenney, Jane Mell and Wendy Zimmermann. 1989. "Differential Treatment Between Hispanic and Anglo Job Seekers: A Study of Hiring Practices in Two Cities." Report to the GAO. Washington, D.C.: Urban Institute.

DeFreitas, Gregory. 1985. "Ethnic Differentials in Unemployment among Hispanic Americans." In *Hispanics in the U.S. Economy*, edited by George T. Borjas and Marta Tienda. New York: Academic Press.

Hakken, Jon. 1979. "Discrimination Against Chicanos in the Dallas Rental Housing Market: An Experimental Extension of the Housing Market Practice Survey." Washington, D.C.: U.S. Department of Housing and Urban Development.

Harrison, Bennett, and Barry Bluestone. 1988. *The Great U-Turn*. New York: Basic Books, Inc.

Holzer, Harry J. 1988. "Search Method Use by Unemployed Youth." *Journal of Labor Economics*, 6:1 (January): 1-20.

James, Franklin, Betty McCummings, and Eileen Tynan. 1984. *Minorities in the Sunbelt*. New Brunswick, N.J.: Center for Urban Policy Research.

Kish, Leslie. 1967. *Survey Sampling*. New York: John Wiley & Sons.

Mangum, Stephen L. 1982. "Job Search: A Review of the Literature." Prepared under contract for the Office of Research and Development, Employment and Training

Administration, Department of Labor. Salt Lake City and San Francisco: Olympus Research Centers.

Marlin, John, Immanuel Ness, and Stephen Collins. 1986. *Book of World City Rankings*. New York: Free Press, pp. 22, 69.

Reimers, Cordella W. 1985. "A Comparative Analysis of the Wages of Hispanics, Blacks, and non-Hispanic Whites." In *Hispanics in the U.S. Economy*, edited by George T. Borjas and Marta Tienda. Orlando: Academic Press.

Rudnitsky, Howard. 1989. "Down and Out in L.A." *Forbes* 144:10 (Oct. 30): 65.

Snedecor, George, and William Cochran. 1967. *Statistical Methods*, 6th edition. Ames, Iowa: Iowa University Press.

Standard and Poor. 1987. *Register of Corporations, Directors, and Executives*, vol. 1. New York: Standard and Poor.

U.S. Department of Labor, Bureau of Labor Statistics. 1989. *Employment and Earnings*, vol. 36, no. 1. Washington, D.C.: U.S. Department of Labor, Bureau of Labor Statistics, January.

_____. 1990. *Unemployment in States and Local Areas, January-November 1989*. Washington, D.C.: U.S. Department of Labor, Bureau of Labor Statistics, January.

_____. 1989. *Handbook of Labor Statistics, Bulletin 2340.* Washington, D.C.: U.S. Government Printing Office, August.

_____. 1989. *Unemployment in State and Local Areas, January - December 1988.* Washington, D.C.: U.S. Department of Labor, Bureau of Labor Statistics, February.

U.S. General Accounting Office. 1988. "Justice Issues." *Transition Series*, GAO/OCG-89-13TR. Washington, D.C.: U.S. Government Printing Office, November.

Vroman, Wayne, and Susan Vroman. 1989. "International Trade and Money Wage Growth in the 1980's." Washington, D.C.: Urban Institute.

Wienk, Ronald E., C.E. Reid, J.C. Simonson, and F.J. Eggers. 1979. "Measuring Housing Discrimination in American Housing Markets: The Housing Market Practices Survey." Washington, D.C.: Department of Housing and Urban Development.

Yinger, John. 1989. "Estimating Variation in Discriminatory Behavior." Research Report no. 4, Contract HC-5811. Washington, D.C.: Urban Institute.

_____. 1988. "Measuring Discrimination in Housing Availability." Research Report no. 2, Contract HC-5811. Washington, D.C.: Urban Institute.